Find Your Market-Oriented Competitive Advantage

Markku Vierula

Find Your Market-Oriented Competitive Advantage

A Toolkit for Strategy and Branding

Markku Vierula
Vierula Consulting oy
Helsinki, Etelä-Suomi, Finland

The book was originally published in Finnish under the title "Löydä kilpailuetusi: Käsikirja strategian ja brändin kehittämiseen" in 2021 by the publisher Kauppakamari

Translation from the Finnish language edition: "Löydä kilpailuetusi – käsikirja strategian ja brändin kehittämiseen" by Markku Vierula, © Author 2021. Published by Kauppakamari. All Rights Reserved.

ISBN 978-3-031-71662-1   ISBN 978-3-031-71663-8 (eBook)
https://doi.org/10.1007/978-3-031-71663-8

© Vierula Consulting 2024
This work is subject to copyright. All rights are solely and exclusively licensed by the Publisher, whether the whole or part of the material is concerned, specifically the rights of translation, reprinting, reuse of illustrations, recitation, broadcasting, reproduction on microfilms or in any other physical way, and transmission or information storage and retrieval, electronic adaptation, computer software, or by similar or dissimilar methodology now known or hereafter developed.
The use of general descriptive names, registered names, trademarks, service marks, etc. in this publication does not imply, even in the absence of a specific statement, that such names are exempt from the relevant protective laws and regulations and therefore free for general use.
The publisher, the authors and the editors are safe to assume that the advice and information in this book are believed to be true and accurate at the date of publication. Neither the publisher nor the authors or the editors give a warranty, expressed or implied, with respect to the material contained herein or for any errors or omissions that may have been made. The publisher remains neutral with regard to jurisdictional claims in published maps and institutional affiliations.

This Springer imprint is published by the registered company Springer Nature Switzerland AG
The registered company address is: Gewerbestrasse 11, 6330 Cham, Switzerland

If disposing of this product, please recycle the paper.

CONTENTS

FOREWORD xii
A radical piece xiii
The book is a toolkit xv
Main objective and milestones xvii

PART I:
TOWARDS A COMPETITIVE EDGE 1

HOPES AND CASTLES IN THE AIR 2
The big market changers 3

"LET'S JUST MAKE THE CHANGE
– IF ONLY WE KNEW HOW!" 4
Lack of competitive edge shows 5
Vectors pulling in different directions 7
Customer value is visible to the customer 7

TOWARDS THE BASICS OF THE COMPETITIVE EDGE TOOLKIT 8
Background 8
Forget Sun Tzu 9
Summaries and guidelines 13

PART II:
FIND YOUR MARKET-ORIENTED COMPETITIVE ADVANTAGE 14

WHAT IS A COMPETITIVE ADVANTAGE? 19

Strategic marketing skills are key 21
Framework for the toolkit 22
The three pillars 24
The 4Ps model turns into a market-oriented 4 Cs model 26
Moving on to the toolkits department 27
Strategic directions 28

SET OF TOOLKITS 29

Direction 1: The company creates something radical and new 29
Direction 2: The company perceives a change in the industry - and shapes the business to fit it 30
Direction 3: The company creates something incrementally new 31
Direction 4: The company recreates itself 32
Direction 5: Focusing 32
Direction 6: Market shaping 33
Direction 7: Business as usual 33
Three different competitive advantages 34
    Strategic competitive advantage 35
    Decisive competitive advantage 35
    Differentiating competitive advantage 36
Starting points for creating a competitive advantage 37
    Goal-oriented 37
    Market-oriented 38
    Resource-oriented 38
Assess the degree of urgency 39
Also make use of classic toolkits 40
Positioning to near and far 40

FINDING A COMPETITIVE ADVANTAGE IN THE COMPANY'S RESOURCES 42

From competitiveness to competitive advantage 43
Competitive advantage through a product or service 43
Core capabilities and core competences 45
Competence design 46
Practising the pattern game 47
Competitiveness already exists 48
Six steps in the search for a resource-based competitive advantage 49
Start from customer needs 50
Six steps to finding your competitive advantage 51
Five criteria for a competitive advantage 52

CONCRETE BUSINESS EXAMPLES 53

Xx B2C examples 55
XX B2B examples 66
Other company examples 79

COMPETITIVE ADVANTAGE PUT INTO PRACTICE 83

Competitive advantage is at the heart of strategy 84
    Small business elevator pitch 84
    Growth requires a strategy 86
    Heart and brain 86

COMPETITIVE ADVANTAGE AS A DRIVER FOR ORGANISATIONAL DEVELOPMENT 87

Are we doing the right things? 88

A BRAND IS A JOINT CREATION BY THE CUSTOMER AND THE COMPANY 92

Defining the brand 92
Not everyone can be a brand 93
Re-branding an existing business 95
The fast lane to branding opens up
with a competitive advantage 96
Integrate the whole organization with a brand 98
Make the brand a band 99
Barriers to change 100

COMMUNICATION 101

How to write an elevator pitch 102
Summary 107

PART III:
FOOD FOR THOUGHT 109

INNOVATION REQUIRES CREATIVITY 110

Creative work is important 110
We need business creativity 110
Wide-ranging creative competence 111
Creativity stinks of sweat 111
Ideas that create value 113
Eurekas and relevations 113
What does Professor Alf Rehn think? 114

COMPETITIVE ADVANTAGE IS AN UMBRELLA TERM FOR CURRENT TRENDS AND MEANS 115

Competitive advantage comes in trough the back door 116

WELL-KNOWN STRATEGY TOOLKITS 118

1. Toolkits to improve efficiency 118
2. Toolkits for creating something new 118
3. Toolkits for resource development 120
4. Positioning toolkits 121
Summary 122

HOW THE TOOLKIT WAS CREATED 124

No common plot 124
Kotler´s ball wall as the basis of the toolkit 125
Dozens of definitions 126
Searching for companies 127
The ABC method as the basis of the toolkit 127
From toolkit to book 131

A FINE CONCLUSION TO THE TOOLKIT 132

Author and developer of the toolkit 133
Thanks 134
Source list 135
The Book blurbs 142

FOREWORD

The visual of an egg and sperm is probably familiar to everyone. The one where a couple of hundred sperm try to reach the egg with their tails wagging. We know the inevitable outcome of the relentless sperm race: only one will reach the goal and fertilise the egg. Everyone else is a loser.

Businesses face the same competitive situation. The supply of services and products exceeds demand in every sector and segment. There is less demand than supply. When, from the buyers' point of view, the supply is also generic and similar to everything else, price competition is created. Distinction from competitors is often built by sugar-coating products and services with contemporary terms. However, from a market perspective, supply tends to look similar. Products and services for which there is more supply than demand have no particular commercial value. The price level is often determined by the lowest price on the market.

Competition between companies is fierce. As a result, the sea turns blood red. Yet, someone always succeeds. Just like someone hitting the jackpot in the lottery, slot machines, or online poker. Despite the success of one, most businesses often take a beating, so to say – when one wins, the others lose. This is an endless zero-sum game where no new value is created, and the cake does not grow in size. Companies are pecking each other to death. There is a risk of slipping into price competition or getting lost in the grey mass.

 When one company digs a hole and another fills it, no new value is created.

During the gold rush of the 19th century, it wasn't just the gold panners who won. The winners were also those entrepreneurs who knew how to create value for the prospectors who had moved to California: selling toolkits, services, clothing, and equipment. During the next wave, the winners were the far-sighted ones who based their businesses on those who had prospered directly or indirectly from gold: banks, creators of services, and builders of transport links and infrastructure. New value was created and business ideas developed. There was plenty of increased value and wealth to share. Businesses and communities prospered. In today's California, Silicon Valley is said to be the modern-day succession of gold miners.

The main aim of this book is to help companies and organisations to find and create their own competitive edge. The traditional idea is to try to beat your competitor. The key to this book is to find value in what the customer does and needs – and to create a competitive edge based on that. The main thing is not to compete against another company or to try to defeat the competitor. When companies focus primarily on identifying customer needs and creating solutions, rather than following the competition, they create a richer and more diverse range of products and services. A wider selection will also help buyers to better understand their own problems.

A radical piece

The idea of market orientation – rather than product orientation – at the heart of this book is a game changer. It represents extremely radical thinking. Market orientation in this book is not an old acquaintance walking in with new sales trousers on. Market orientation is a completely new perspective. A paradigm shift.

In business, there is a lot of talk about customer orientation. However, from the point of view of the market orientation discussed in this book, today's customer orientation is fundamentally product-oriented, which is the opposite of market orientation. Product orientation is thinking, 'We have these products, who would they suit best?' You first have the product, and then you find the objects to sell them to. Product orientation does not include the idea that before products and services were developed, there was an insight into the customer's need for the product. Market-oriented customer focus is at the heart of this book.

The importance of competitive advantage for a company's success can hardly be disputed. For sole entrepreneurs, micro-enterprises and small SMEs, the competitive edge, or competitive advantage, is the company's strategy: the silver bullet that allows it to attract customers without having to compete on price. A competitive edge is the factor that allows a company to take control of its future and dodge the blows of its competitors. A competitive edge allows a company to change its pricing. When a firm competes by creating value, it avoids direct price competition. Value pricing is more profitable and less exposed to price competition. A market-oriented company rejects the idea that a company thrives on sales. A market-oriented business needs sales skills, of course, but it thrives on value creation and the margins that come from it.

'The anatomy of a good strategy' does not exist. Personally, I see a competitive edge at the heart of a successful strategy. When a company finds a competitive edge, this acts as a silver bullet.

Competitive edge is a #silverbullet

- a competitive edge is a strategic policy from the company's management
- a competitive edge is the thing that enables a company to operate in a hyper-competitive market
- a competitive edge is the basis on which a company develops its collective competence.

As we can see, a competitive edge permeates the whole organisation. Thus, it provides an opportunity to create a common script both internally and externally.

For a larger SME, a competitive edge is the cornerstone of strategy. Or the core of the success of a product or service. Finding a competitive edge enables a company to develop its business in a focused, long-term way. When a company delivers value to its customers, it has the opportunity to move from being a subcontractor to a partner. As a partner, the interaction deepens, which in turn allows a better understanding of the customer – and further development.

A company that has found a competitive edge can be compared to a person who is attractive, handsome or beautiful, desirable, social, influential, and successful. Who wouldn't want to be one!

The need to find a competitive edge applies not only to businesses but also to the products and services they represent and to public administration operators. With a practical approach, this book's lessons also encourage you to find the competitive advantage of your products and services. 'Practical' in this context means that the book not only tells you *what* to do (as most literature does) but also gives you solutions on *how* to do it. This book includes both sides to make it easier to reach the desired results.

The book is a toolkit

In fact, the whole book is a toolkit from which each reader can choose the toolkits that suit their own situation and apply them as they see fit. At the heart of the book is the Find Your Competitive Advantage™ toolkit that I have created. It is also unique on an international scale: as far as I know, there is no other similar toolkit. As the developer of the toolkit and the author of this book, I have practised what I preach: created something new and unique.

This book replaces the product-, production- and price-oriented mindset with a market- and customer-oriented mindset. In this book, for example, the word customer value does not mean how valuable the customer is to the company – as it is still often understood – but rather what value the company can bring to the customer. When you can deliver superior value, your company's emotional, social and economic well-being is on firmer footing.

Competitive advantage is not a de facto guarantee of success. You also need a business model to run your business. A good idea needs a functional implementation. A competitive edge is the heart and brains of a business, whether you are a sole entrepreneur or with a start-up or a larger company that has been around for a while.

There is no doubt about the importance of competitive advantage for a company's success. Business books and textbooks, researchers, professors, various publications and studies, and gurus working in business development all emphasize that competitive advantage is the cornerstone of success, the most important investment a company can make. A competitive edge is at the heart of a business idea and strategy.

Each year, strategy is the subject of a truckload of articles and literature. Over the decades, the head of this line of trucks has disappeared from sight. There are fewer guides that even attempt to highlight how to create a competitive edge. Toolkits for finding the competitive edge – at least ones not based on market-oriented thinking – do not even exist, as far as I know. Not to mention a heavy toolkit. Competitive edge is discussed for what it is, but there is hardly any discussion of how to create it. Of course, there are individual models of how to find your competitive edge, but I have not encountered anything like the one you have in your hands.

The international bestseller *Blue Ocean Strategy* (2005) by **W. Chan Kim and Renée Mauborgne** excellently sells the idea of avoiding competition and moving to the blue ocean. The *Blue Ocean Shift* (2017) by the same authors encourages you to find ideas that avoid price competition and allow the company to price its offering based on the value it delivers. Author and business guru **Simon Sinek** is dedicated to speaking, writing, training and consulting on the meaning of companies. He has brilliantly put forward the idea that instead of saying "what" a company does, it should say "why" it does what it does. In his most recent book *Infinite Game* (2018), Sinek writes about the importance of creating innovations and how following the competition is not essential to their creation: it is important to understand that competition never ends, but that creating something new is the key to success for the company, its target groups and stakeholders. The organisational development bible *Reinventing Organizations* (2014) by **Frederic Laloux** mentions competitive advantage but does not go deeper into the topic.

In **Michael E. Porter's** classic work *Competitive Advantage* (1985), it is estimated that competitive advantage can be a focusing strategy, a price competition or cost leadership strategy, or a differentiation strategy.

In the literature on strategy, competitive edge and how to create it is often talked about in whispers, and most of the time even more quietly.

This book and the Find Your Competitive Advantage™ toolkit at its heart aims to be the exception that proves the rule. The book is not content to just hover around the concept of competitive advantage. With my book, I stand on the shoulders of these giants and try to reach the next level. I will continue where the above-mentioned masters (and many others) left off with their excellent books.

Professor of Entrepreneurship **Arto Lahti** and management consultant and non-fiction writer **Timo Rope** highlight the importance and role of strategic marketing, especially from a management perspective. Rope sees strategic marketing as a skill that helps a company create a competitive edge. He sees competitive advantage as a key objective of business development. He defines strategy as "ensuring the success of a company's solutions through the selection of a playing field and the development of a competitive advantage".

Main objective and milestones

The main aim of this book is to help your product, service, company, and organisation to create a differentiating competitive advantage. In order to reach the main objective, milestones are also needed. Challenging your own fixed mindset, broadening your thinking, and understanding the importance of creativity are these milestones. This book offers something on them, too. Market-oriented thinking, strategic marketing skills, and business creativity function as the angle grinder, the wrecking ball and the diamond cutter.

The Find Your Competitive Edge toolkit has been created using a "practice to model" methodology. Years ago, I started to keenly read studies on the competitive advantages, business ideas, and quality of strategies of (also Finnish) companies. I had a lightbulb moment when I realised that only

very few

companies have a compelling, distinctive and clear competitive advantage or strategy. Once again, I started to revisit the literature on strategy and follow the debate around strategy. The importance of competitive advantage was underlined in all of them. At the Nordic Business Forum in Helsinki (October 2021), Professor **Gary Hamel** 2018 highlighted that innovation is the most critical competitive edge in today's business world.

In this book, a closely related concept to the concept of innovation mentioned by Hamel is competitive advantage. Once a company has created a competitive advantage, it has also created an innovation.

Despite the importance of competitive advantage, there are surprisingly few competitive advantages. The concept of a competitive edge may not be well known. As a term, it is often mixed with competitiveness and competitive assets. Or people can't get a grip on it. They don't want to think about it. Creating it seems challenging.

Who knows.

I started wondering whether I might be able to create a "how to find your competitive edge" toolkit. So, I got down to business. I studied the strategies of international companies. I looked into academic research. My observation was that competitive advantages are not found just like that. I examined the business ideas, competitive advantages, visions, missions, and strategies of Finnish companies. I quickly discovered (although I had already empirically established this in my practical work) that the situation is this: competitive advantages and strategies are at a modest level. There were exceptions, of course, when I first learned to identify a good business idea and really combed through and looked for them.

I recorded and analysed the good and excellent competitive advantages, business ideas, and strategies I found. I realized that they all involved creating something new, fresh, and extraordinary.

After much thought and work, I realised that I would build my models on excellent business examples. All the products, services, and companies I analysed were Finnish. The literature I read was international.

The aim of the book is

- to help people considering starting a business, sole entrepreneurs, and micro-enterprises find a competitive edge in their field
- to help a growing SME to find a competitive edge for its product, service, and/or business and build a strategy around it
- to help public administrations to find their competitive edge (market-oriented thinking brings a fresh and inspiring perspective to the development of their activities)
- to provide concrete examples of what market-oriented thinking and doing is
- to open up strategic marketing skills to management (market-oriented operations require an understanding of strategic marketing) and make it a familiar area of expertise for owners, boards, and management
- to shed light on the concept of competitive edge (as it seems to be difficult to grasp)
- to help businesses to develop and thus contribute to the welfare society.

The shift from product-driven to market-oriented thinking opens up a whole new way of thinking. It's a game changer. This is not a protest book, even if it is (also) provocative. Creating new thinking requires breaking down old, traditional ways of thinking. It may be that the reader may sometimes be annoyed by the style that questions their thinking and reminds them of stagnant ways of doing things. Rubbing people the wrong way has a purpose.

No pain, no gain.

In the modern digital environment, the question of how to scale a business idea is often raised. I have also been asked about that regarding this toolkit. I have answered that it happens in two ways:

- by creating training programmes in both Finnish and English that operate on different platforms
- and by providing ideas and toolkits for other businesses and entrepreneurs to develop their own activities.

I personally consider the latter an important form of scaling. In other words, it means that companies broaden their thinking, get inspiration and ideas for developing their own activities, and that the overall selection is richer as a result.

The sensitive side of the book

This book also has a sensitive side. It wants to stimulate, sensitize, and act as a sparring partner. It is, therefore, a combination of different roles, such as researcher, expert, educator, creative designer, and consultant, all of whom will tell their story from different perspectives. The practical perspective and approach bring out an understanding of the world of work, making it easier to apply what you learn to your own situation and work.

This book can rightly be described as a colouring and development book. That's because I also aim to provide practical guidance and toolkits to stimulate thinking – and also to create new value. The book aims to maintain a Socratic debate; asking questions, refuting beliefs, and offering new perspectives are part of the method. So, the book promotes new creation on two fronts: it tells you why you should do it and gives you ideas on how to do it.

It is also a manifesto for strategic marketing skills. A market-oriented company must understand the philosophical and substantive importance of strategic marketing in business development. Market orientation is a core competence for successful companies.

The book also contains a healthy dose of idealism in thinking that every company has the potential to be the best version of itself. When focusing on the needs of customers and continuing to excel, more original business ideas emerge and mutual competition is reduced. As companies' ability to produce a greater extent of added value improves, so does the well-being of products, services, companies, and organisations.

What you have in your hands is a radical and provocative book – but also a constructive one. It challenges our way of thinking and can, therefore, also irritate the reader. The possible annoyance serves a purpose: this book also wants to induce dopamine production and to give inspiration and a means to create something new.

Book contents

This book implements a department store model: you can enter through several doors. With a long line of readers consisting of professionals and others interested in competitive advantage, all with different levels of expertise and starting knowledge, the content can be approached according to the reader's personal needs.

The book consists of three parts. They form an integrated whole, from value discovery to brand definition and communication planning. I have compressed this whole, which is often divided into several books, into a single book. Part I moves towards competitive advantage. It outlines the landscape ahead and discusses competitive advantages and business strategies.

Part II focuses on finding a competitive advantage. I will present in detail the seven strategic directions from which you can seek your own competitive advantage. I present three different definitions of competitive advantages at different levels. I also consider how the skills and resources already present in a company can be used to create a competitive edge. After all, there is a huge variety of skills in companies. The directions act like a kaleidoscope, offering different views.

Part II includes company visits to xx companies. I will not present any examples like Amazon or Zalando. Partly because they are of little use to SMEs as examples for development. Classic examples such as Apple, Tesla, JPMorgan Chase & Co, and ExxonMobil do not offer SMEs anything to identify with. I feel that it is useless to give advice like "think like Steve Jobs" or "act like Elon Musk". They operate on a completely different scale from SMEs in all respects. They are also very unfamiliar as role models for smaller companies.

'The anatomy of a good strategy' does not exist. Personally, I see a competitive edge at the heart of a successful strategy. When a company finds a competitive edge, this acts as a silver bullet.

The so-called company visits in the book demonstrate the strategic orientation of each company on the basis of the directions given by the toolkit. I will briefly describe the business idea and business model and use them to shed light on the company's competitive advantage or business idea. I will also define the strategic direction based on which the competitive advantage has been created and which of the three competitive advantages (discussed later in the book) the company has. We will also look at the role of communication as a success factor. Some of the business cases may be familiar to you, but most are new acquaintances. Some of the companies presented have the potential to become major global players. All the companies are Finnish. My view is that companies that are unknown to the reader offer the opportunity to analyse them without preconceived ideas. What is essential is showcasing the competitive advantage. In this respect, Finnish companies are in the same position as any other product or company operating in a competitive market.

Competitive advantage must also be translated into practice. That operation will be examined in Part III. The topics covered in this section include brand definition and how to use a brand to holistically integrate the company around its customers.

Even the best business idea cannot exist without good communication. This book, therefore, also looks at the communication of an organisation that has found its competitive advantage, both internally and externally. The role of communication, including the importance of being able to dramatize a message and make an excellent competitive edge visible, cannot be overlooked when creating a viable and successful business idea. Part III also provides some toolkit examples on how to turn a generic, product-oriented promise into a market-oriented elevator pitch. In a media-driven environment, companies also compete at the level of communication. Success in the media noise is one part of the success of a successful business. On the other hand, once a company has found its competitive edge, it has its communication outlined – both internally and externally.

Organisational development as a whole is a topical and important issue in the present day when individual development, the need for change, operating in networks, and change management are the big trends. We are in the turmoil of change and looking for direction. Competitive advantage enters the debate here as a signpost and a carrier rocket.

Part III brings together thought-provoking themes. New, innovative products, services, or businesses are not created by thinking the same way as before. To create something new, you first need to break down the barriers of thinking. It's not enough to decorate a room with new colours; you need to rethink the whole room. The thinking behind the thinking needs to be reformed.

Creativity also has its own chapter. Let's call it #businesscreativity. Creating something new, be it a better product or a revolutionary innovation, is not possible in a crowded market without creative talent. Encoded in the DNA of this book is the idea that beating your rival is not a fruitful starting point. It is more important to create new value to meet customer needs. This, in turn, requires the creation of something new, which equals the search for and discovery of competitive advantage. It's challenging – but just finding a rough idea for a competitive edge provides inspiration and new perspectives.

Disclaimer: this only applies to companies that want to develop something new with a market-oriented approach.

PART I: TOWARDS A COMPETITIVE EDGE

! **I wanted to create a book that is a game changer.**

Many people look away when the talk turns to a competitive edge. We don't – instead, we keep our eyes on the prize and focus 100% on a competitive edge.

Competitive edge is at the heart of each product, service, company, and organisational strategy. Achieving competitive advantage is the ultimate goal of business development. Strategy is a *heavy* word. From a company's point of view, strategy contains all the policies and decisions that the company decides to implement in order to succeed in competitive arenas. There is strategic leadership and strategic thinking. There are several strategic schools of thought. There is a huge amount of material under the heading 'strategic literature' (this book is one of them). Strategy as a term is open to interpretation – and that is why it has remained vague in many respects. When you want to emphasise the importance of a decision, it is called 'strategic'. There are also strategic media choices, strategic leadership, strategic content, and strategic advertising. Strategic this and that. Someone has said that a carpet in the lobby of a company is a strategic choice. When everything is strategic, I think a lot of people lose their grip on strategy.

HOPES AND CASTLES IN THE AIR

"We want to grow by 35 per cent."
 "We strive to be the best overall supplier."
"We want to be thought leaders."
"Our aim is to be number one in our chosen segment."
"We offer high-quality pioneering services."
"At the heart of our strategy is a questioning transformational-disruptive renewal." (If you want to put the strategy in a contemporary dress.)

These are some typical examples of strategies. There are a lot of them, and they sound like positive phrases. They use adjectives that are nice, contemporary, and well-meaning. They are certainly familiar to all of us. Many of them have probably been developed by competent professionals, but the competence is not articulated or is, so to speak, buried in the action. But when you look more closely at the strategies, you discover that they are merely hopes and ambitions. As such, quite respectable. But they lack the means and the know-how to achieve those strategic hopes and ambitions. These strategic orientations do not ignite flames of enthusiasm among staff. It is difficult to formulate a sales pitch that appeals to the customer from the "we want to grow by 35%" strategy. In it, the potential buyer does not see their role as anything other than an object of sale. A company that offers "high-quality pioneering services" should think more deeply about for whom, at what stage of the customer journey, and what value that high-quality pioneering service delivers. When the starting point is "tilted", it also produces tilted activity in the value chain. This type of strategy also makes it difficult to plan and implement, for example, strategic communication.

Often, corporate strategies are like late autumn days: joyless, grey, and foggy. They do not answer the question "what value is created and for whom" – let alone talk about competitive advantage. Often, you see strategies that spend more time on visualisation than on the core content of the strategy itself. A visualised road map to success may look lofty, but without a competitive edge, it works as well as a guitar out of tune.

© Vierula Consulting 2024
M. Vierula, *Find Your Market-Oriented Competitive Advantage*,
https://doi.org/10.1007/978-3-031-71663-8_1

Strategies could be described more as aspirations, expressions of hopes, or fantasies. Does the term "strategy-ish" better describe the poor state of strategies? They have the right idea but are often empty in terms of content. By strategy-ish, I also mean the classic PowerPoint presentation with the intriguing title "Strategy 2023-2027", which, in reality, is a multi-page stack of papers that can be read by staff on the intranet. Or the leaflet that the management team forgot the day after it was written. "Strategies haven't been a hindrance to us in the past, either," said one expert about his company's strategy.

The big market changers

The world and markets have become more digital and globalised, and competition between companies has become 'hyper competition'. The internet, search engines, and smartphones are the big market changers. We have entered an era of knowledge work and networked operations. The value of work is less and less created in a linear fashion, as in an industrial plant, where at one end, the production materials are put on a conveyor belt and at the other end, the finished products are assembled, packaged and stored.

Value and results are being in more complex ways as the end result of collaboration between a team and different talents and networks. You could say that

 whereas in the industrial era, the factory was an integrated production unit, in the modern era, the production unit is the company's team – and its networks.

"LET'S JUST MAKE THE CHANGE – IF ONLY WE KNEW HOW!"

Change and renewal are talked about every day. They come up in many different ways, in many different contexts and forms. This is reflected in research results and encounters. When a management consultant asks the management of a company in a meeting, "What is your business idea?", there is no clear answer. Just try to sell change management services when you can't find the element on top of the company's foundation that could be used as a basis for change and growth.

Where there is demand for change, there are also agents of change. Lean, service design, content marketing, branding, and growth hacking are examples of the ways in which change and development are sought. Good and necessary skills, all in all. However, they, or their buyers, have one common flaw. They are all linked to product-oriented thinking. Product-oriented thinking is so firmly part of the tradition that even the most modern methods and their applications are its direct descendants.

"Here are our products – how could we sell them?" thinking has given rise to whole schools of thought whose expertise is being used to address this industrial-age question.

The supply of services is naturally demand-driven. When demand is product-driven, services are also product-driven. When companies declare that their aim is to find new customers, but the cake doesn't grow, you know what happens when there is far more supply than demand. Price competition tempts a large number of companies because what is abundantly available has little commercial value.

Finding a competitive edge enriches supply. An individual company builds its pricing based on the value produced (and avoids competitive pricing).

 Product-oriented thinking is so firmly part of the tradition that even the most modern methods are its direct descendants.

© Vierula Consulting 2024
M. Vierula, *Find Your Market-Oriented Competitive Advantage*,
https://doi.org/10.1007/978-3-031-71663-8_2

The same product orientation is also reflected in start-ups. Studies show that the vast majority of companies starve when trying to cross the valley of death. They receive the kiss of death because their idea doesn't work. Or the target group is not reached. Or the idea did not find a target group. So, the depths of despair also threaten start-ups even if they can be judged to be operating in a modern way, in a modern environment.

Lack of competitive edge shows

The lack of competitive advantage has led to some companies slipping into price competition – or being stuck in the grey mass. It is a matter of opinion which is worse for an individual company.

Another remnant of industrial thinking is that competitive advantage is not understood as a term. Or it is misunderstood. That's why competitive advantage may not be given the time – and thought – it deserves. 'There are two kinds of things, important and urgent', a saying goes. In those situations, urgency often wins. Competitive advantage is the underdog in this race.

Of course, many companies have considered the concept of a competitive edge. When a company mentally lists seven competitive advantages for its service, it is a sign that there is no specific competitive advantage. There are only the elements for creating a competitive advantage. Another display of sloppy competitive edge thinking can be seen when a company identifies as competitive advantages the same factors as its best competitors. Or the company lists the generic success factors of the industry or segment as its competitive advantages.

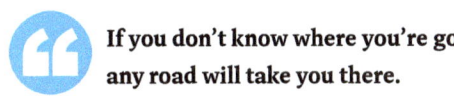

> **If you don't know where you're going,
> any road will take you there.**
>
> Alice in Wonderland, Lewis Carroll

The lack of a competitive edge has also often led to the development of a company through various secondary lessons. Often, the tool of choice is the familiar "cheese slicer". It is not known to bring about growth and development.

A competitive edge is a game changer. In companies where competitive advantage is defined or embedded in the business idea and business model, it acts as a common script that is consistently implemented at all levels. This competitive advantage and the strategy that has been built on it are visible and continue to have an impact on the employee and customer experience. Research shows that the competitive edge, mission and compelling purpose included in companies' resources and operating models help them to operate more efficiently and successfully.

 There is no anatomy of a successful strategy in the strategy literature. But it recognises that finding a competitive advantage is the optimal way to ensure success. This book puts competitive advantage at the heart of success.

A company without a competitive advantage is like a fallow field. There might be all sorts of things growing.

It's like a gun without a bullet.

A sentence without a thought.

It's like trying to start a moped without spark plugs.

 "Competitive advantage is at the heart of the success of a company operating in a free market".

According to Professor **Don E. Schultz,** the whole organisation must be wrapped around the customers (and stakeholders). In the lectures and training courses I have given on integration, promoting the team play of different functions, I have seen and heard the need to promote team play, especially at the operational level. It is difficult to integrate measures and shape an organisation in the direction of promoting team play if the company does not have a defined common script, a shared idea of the purpose of its operations. According to Schultz, organisations often have the know-how to do better. He says it's just scattered across the organisation.

Vectors pulling in different directions

In the traditional model, separate objectives and strategies are created for each function. When there is no common thread, there are vectors pulling in different directions. Sales have their own objectives and strategies, as do marketing and communications. The main reason for this disharmony is that the company does not have a common script or a common thread to guide everything it does, also at the level of functions and objectives.

We live in an era of knowledge work and networks. In addition to our own specific skills, we need to understand customers, supply chains, and value chains. The number of stakeholders can be considerable. This also requires the development of shared competencies within the company. A competitive edge helps to organise, manage, and focus this work.

Customer value is visible to the customer

Customer value is often seen as a term that refers to how much a customer generates money for the company. To put it more precisely, this is how managers and staff in production-oriented companies think. Those are the operators who think, "Here are our products, who can we sell them to?" Of course, this financial aspect is also important in business planning, but since the money for the business comes from customers, you need to be able to see the dark side of the moon, so to speak.

In market-oriented thinking, customer value also means how a product, service, or company can create value for the customer. Value can be economic, social, functional, ethical, image-related, and so on. It can be any of these elements or various combinations of them. The key is that it adds value to the customer's own actions. In a free market and hyper-competitive environment, a successful business is driven by delivering value to another business or consumer. The starting point is the customer, not the company providing the products or services. There is no ready-made model for success. It cannot be found in a spreadsheet. New things are created by creating new things.

TOWARDS THE BASICS OF THE COMPETITIVE EDGE TOOLKIT

Background

"Traditionally, competence has been considered to be a thorough knowledge of products/services and the ability to improve them a little."

Many companies are still guided by this thinking. This way of doing things has had its time and place in the development of industrialisation. In-depth knowledge of products and services is often a skill that is passed down through tradition. The canon is still very much present.

The widely quoted business legend Peter Drucker wrote this decades ago:

 Managers are concerned with doing things right.
Leaders are concerned with doing the right things.
I have extended to it: True leaders are concerned with
doing the right things right.

Peter Drucker

Let's unravel Drucker's already classic idea: We know how to do *things right* because we have the knowledge, skills, and technical know-how. We're good at doing the *right things* (products, marketing communications, or sales).

Many companies are doing things right, but are they doing the right things? Can we do what Peter Drucker asks of true leaders: do the right things right?

True leaders want the right things done the right way.

Businesses are on the threshold of changes that cannot be solved by tinkering with current operations. The Finnish Mikko Kosonen echoes Drucker's sentiment by suggesting that organisations do not die because they do the wrong things but because they continue to do the things that were once right for too long.

© Vierula Consulting 2024
M. Vierula, *Find Your Market-Oriented Competitive Advantage*,
https://doi.org/10.1007/978-3-031-71663-8_3

So, change and implementation alone is not the answer; you have to go to the heart of the change.

So, what is the philosopher's stone? Where to find the plot for the right way?

Fixed costs are within an organisation. The results are outside the organisation, in the customers and the customers' needs, Peter Drucker reminds us. The customer pays the salaries of the staff. When Drucker says that marketing and innovation are the most important skills, I think he means that in order to succeed, a company must focus on finding new, superior value and communicating it to the market. Or, as Seth Godin has written, "Stop advertising and start innovating." The idea could also be clarified with this idea from Godin: *"Don't find customers for your products, find products for your customers."*

Business strategies are often shaped by aspirations, as I said earlier: "We want this, we want that." The competitiveness of a company, on the other hand, is often developed by studying the activities of competitors. When a company adds an extra item to its offering, it will soon be offered by its competitor as well, "so as not to be left behind". Strategy is explained by what competitors do, not by the value the customer gets. In many cases, strategies and offerings are becoming clones of each other. There is no significant novelty to be gained by following the actions of a competitor and developing one's own activities on that basis. When development is industry-based, new thinking does not emerge. You could compare this to the life of a pea: when a pea lives its whole life in a pea pod, there is no other reality than the green reality.

Forget Sun Tzu

The basis of strategy is very often the same as the doctrine of how to win a war. Strategic thinking, along with its toolkits, has reinforced this thinking. **Sun Tzu's** *The Art of War,* written in ancient China before the dawn of time, is often used as a basic strategic work, referred to in the context of business strategy. In war, this thinking is beneficial. History tells us that at the Battle of Trafalgar in 1805, Admiral **Nelson** defeated the French fleet. We Finns know that Finland stopped the Red Army's major offensive in the defensive victory of Tali-Ihantala. As I write this, Ukraine is bravely defending itself against Russia's unjustified and brutal aggression. These were and are battles against an enemy.

In today's business world, companies are fighting new battles that require new ways of thinking and breaking away from the old. The fact that even a company thinks primarily of defeating its competitor leads to inbred thinking, a weakening of the genome. Competitors are being watched more and more closely: now that they have made that move, should we make it as well? Now that they are expanding their distribution chain to new areas, how do we react to that move? Should we also offer that service?

As organisations follow what others are doing and develop their activities through them, companies increasingly become copies of each other. The offering is narrowing and becoming increasingly homogeneous. The abundant market is becoming even more crowded with similar products and services. More and more clones are being created that are indistinguishable from each other. This means that a company slips into price competition or gets lost in the grey mass. There are many products and services on offer, but very few of them make it to brands. It's fair to say: if you do what everyone else does, you have no strategy.

A company's success is based on the success of its customers and its ability to create value for them. Shouldn't the core of strategy then be the needs of the customers; both their articulated messages and the tacit ones that a sensitive, perceptive, and even intuitive company could use as the basis for a strategy? Of course, it is good to know what your competitor is doing, but that is not the starting point for market-oriented development. Let the customer be a source of inspiration!

The word *change* in its various forms has been a buzzword for years. Everyone has heard the term *change management* a million times. The expression *the need for change* has also become familiar. Then there is a whole series of different sentences repeating that word in different senses: Change is necessary. Change in sales. Change is an opportunity.

Of course, changes have been planned and made. At strategy days and seminars, there is often a stirring consensus on the need for change. It is easy for the audience to get carried away by an enthusiastic speech using positive words – and then find out the next day that it didn't really mean anything. Is it change for change's sake? Or because it's talked about so much?

There is trade around change; some are offering, and others are buying. It's easy to buy the high-minded talk as a beautiful hope for a better tomorrow. The belief that the sun will rise is strong. Without a fundamental rethink, reality will hit the fan like a nasty turd.

It is also said that culture eats strategy for breakfast. There are many different types of renovation crews in companies. ICT systems and software are maintained and updated. The ergonomic facilities of offices are analysed. Someone bears the glad tidings of digitalisation, and the internal team wants to raise the spirit of togetherness, along the lines of "Hey everyone, let's all pull together!" The third and fourth person is already preparing a sales pitch for what the company needs next.

And then you hear it again:

"Yeah, let's make the change!" the management team says enthusiastically in one voice.

"If only we knew how, and what the heck is meant by change," many in the management team wonder to themselves.

Indeed. Many companies have gone through turmoil, even several times. They have tried various options. Fine-tuning feels good when fine-tuning, but it doesn't have much of a bigger or more permanent effect. An endless appetite for change is perhaps followed by a resistance to change.

By this point, the organisation has been modded and prodded. The sales department needs annual maintenance. A repair service will get the job done for a while, but it won't affect the overall picture. The company has tried to make a go of it on its own and sought help from external service providers. It has also been thinking about what the competitors are doing and looking for new dynamics for everyday work. It has also tried to create a sense of community. Many people have experienced a dopamine-induced buzz of well-being when motivation levels have been raised. Next, the visual look has been renewed and the focus has been on sales development. The company has sharpened up. Ruffled its feathers. Individuals and teams have been developed and updated. Semantic acrobatics have been practised.

The company has given less thought to what it is selling. Is its offering up-to-date, distinctive, and appealing?

All the tinkering and tweaking only gets you those breakfasts that culture eats up. Instead of developing the individuals and the company internally, it is worth considering whether the company has thought about from whose point of view it should be developed: Who is the organisation dedicated to? What unique value does it create?

You can't achieve results by focusing on achieving results. The old adage says that doing the right things gets you results. Or, as Peter Drucker said, "The result of the company is outside the company."

Growth is the partner of change. This book is also about change, but in a much more dynamic and radical way than the literature on the subject in general. Renewal is a more precise term than change. Of course, reform requires change. It is not enough to dress the same old things in new clothes. Old chewing gum always tastes old. The change must include a willingness to change the thinking behind the thinking: to push aside production-oriented thinking and bring in market-oriented thinking.

 The world is changing. Today, it is changing faster than ever before. Tomorrow, change will be faster than today.

A competitive advantage cannot be googled. You have to create it yourself. Taking the helm into your own hands is the change and renewal toolkit that allows you to maximize your influence on your own future – and minimize the risk of becoming driftwood. The future does not happen, it is created!

SUMMARIES AND GUIDELINES

- Product-, production- and price-oriented thinking are very much alive in our thinking. This leads to compartmentalisation and the development of separate strategies for each function.

- Corporate strategies are more about what the company is aiming for or what the company is trying to achieve. Much thought has not been given to the means by which companies differentiate themselves from their competitors in order to achieve the objectives they have set.

- A homogeneous supply leads to price competition in a saturated market.

- The means being used to develop businesses are product oriented. When a company focuses on market-oriented development, the familiar ways of developing its operations also take on new value and become even more developmental.

- Companies have technical, knowledge-based, skill-based, and tactical expertise. The conditions for better business are already there.

- By creating unique value for its customers, a company avoids direct price competition.

- A competitive edge is a key investment and the cornerstone of a company's success. It is the sales pitch of a small business and the core of a growing company's strategy.

PART II: FIND YOUR MARKET-ORIENTED COMPETITIVE ADVANTAGE

The time has come to thank the past decades of industrialisation and product orientation.

Moving on to the next era, we welcome organisations that embrace market orientation and want to find a competitive edge.

This section goes to the sources of customer value. We start looking for the value, the competitive advantage, that a company can bring to its customers by providing superior expertise.

The Find Your Competitive Advantage™ toolkit was created using the ABC method, which in a nutshell means academic literature, business concepts, communications, and consulting. I studied the business ideas of dozens and dozens of SMEs. I picked up good competitive advantages and business ideas. I modelled the toolkit using them. For a more detailed description of how the Find YourCompetitive Advantage™ toolkit was created, see the chapter *This is how the toolkit was created* on page 142.

In this chapter:

- I present seven alternative strategic directions.
- I identify three different types of competitive advantages on which a company can start to build its competitive edge.
- I examine how to find and create a competitive advantage from the knowledge, the resources, that already exist in a company.

**The customer employs the company.
And, as is well known, the customer can also dismiss the whole company, up to and including the chairperson of the board. Without dismissal procedure and severance pay.**

DIFFERENTIATE OR DIE
Jack Trout

The non-fiction author and business legend **Jack Trout** talks, consults, and writes about the importance of positioning and differentiation. The quote is the title of one of Trout's most famous books. As you can see from his choice of words, in the title, he offers companies two options: either or.

Differentiation is the more challenging option.

In fact, I will now go even further. Where Trout (often with his colleague **Al Ries**) calls for differentiation through positioning in relation to competitors, I start with a radical and heretical attitude based on customer needs.

Encoded in the DNA of this book is the idea that the most important thing is not to beat the competition but to create value for the customer. This book, therefore, moves with full steam ahead and with the same idea that the Blue Ocean represents: avoid the bloody competition of the Red Ocean and sail the Blue Ocean where there is no direct competition. To get there, you'll need to create something new and unique – an innovation.

Successful business activities are based on creating a hard-to-replicate competitive advantage.
Competitive Advantage, Michael E. Porter

Competitive advantage is at the heart of a firm's performance in competitive markets.

Michael E. Porter argues for a competitive advantage that is difficult to replicate. To achieve a competitive advantage, a company must be able to create superior value for its customers. The value perceived by the customer is achieved either by improving the customer's operations or by reducing the customer's costs.

According to Porter, a company's competitive advantage can be based on three options:

- the company competes in price
- the company focuses or
- the company differentiates.

Here, we concentrate on differentiation. We also raise the issue of focusing, but that also tends to require differentiation. Remember that in this book, differentiation, or the search for differentiation, is based on the value created for customers (not primarily in relation to competitors).

WHAT IS A COMPETITIVE ADVANTAGE?

Understanding business-related concepts and how they relate to each other is often difficult. What is *growth hacking*? How is it different from inbound marketing? It's easy to talk about a brand, but how to create one in practice is another story. And what does business competence mean? What kind of competence is it in practice? What is the relationship between a business idea and a competitive advantage? What about digital transformation? What does a *brand activation director* do? At what stage of the *decision gate* is the prospect? There are many terms, and new ones are emerging all the time. So much so that it takes a lot of effort to stay afloat with them. There are probably as many definers as there are participants in discussions.

Researchers have not reached a consensus on the definition of competitive advantage or a competitive edge. There are several schools of thought. Studies on the concept of a competitive edge link economic success and competitive advantage. One view is that because a company is successful, it has a competitive edge. One school of thought emphasises market orientation in the search for competitive advantage. We will not get bogged down by academic debate here but instead, define competitive edge by outlining its content. Thus, the concept of a competitive edge is more lenient than the terms mentioned above. It's easy to understand once you understand the role and importance of competitive advantage. Here are two definitions of competitive advantage:

Competitive advantage is created when a company implements a value-adding strategy that no current or potential competitor is implementing or has the opportunity to implement (Barney, 1991; Grant, 2008).

Competitive advantage often arises from factors that are difficult to replicate, such as intellectual capital and its management (Barney, 1991). Competitive advantage leads to business success, which is why it is important for entrepreneurs to identify and utilise their competitive advantage.

A related concept to competitive advantage is a business idea:

A successful business idea must be differentiated from competitors by some significant feature, which may be in the product, service, marketing, or manufacturing (Grant, 2008).

© Vierula Consulting 2024
M. Vierula, *Find Your Market-Oriented Competitive Advantage*,
https://doi.org/10.1007/978-3-031-71663-8_4

The importance of competitive advantage at the heart of a successful business is undeniable, as has been shown. Competitive advantage is even widely seen as one of the more essential aspirations of running a business. Business development is a very broad term with multiple dimensions, so we should let competitive advantage crystallise where it should be seen and felt from the customer's perspective:

> **In order to achieve a competitive advantage, a company must be able to create value for its customers. The value perceived by the customer is achieved either by**

- **improving the customer's functions, doing better what they already know, or developing something new for them that they already feel is better than existing solutions; or**
- **by reducing costs for the customer.**

The idea of competitive advantage seems clear, doesn't it? It is not enough for a company to be proud and enthusiastic about its idea or its way of doing things. You have to gain customer acceptance and reach a position where you are more attractive than your competitor – or, in fact, a whole range of competitors. As we said before: expenses are inside the company, cash flow and results are outside. You need to create the kind of value and attractiveness that will drive money toward your business.

Instead of looking for the biggest selling point, we start with the idea of creating superior products that people want to buy.

The definition of competitive advantage is clear, so it is easy to buy into the idea.

"It would be great if we had one. It would solve a lot of problems",
a company representative perhaps thinks.

"We have no competitive advantage. But why is that?"

How can you tell if a company has a competitive advantage and a business idea based on it? What are its characteristics? Here's a five-point checklist:

- innovative
- unique
- problem solver
- feasible
- profitable for both the buyer and the seller.

The importance of competitive advantage as a key success factor is highlighted by studies, professors, consultants, gurus, literature, articles, and successful business leaders.

Competitive advantage emerges as a key element for the business idea, the business model, the company's strategy, and its management.

Competitive advantage is not a de facto guarantee of success. Finding it is about investing in the source of success. In order to be successful, you also need a functional and effective business model. Building a business model is also clearer when competitive advantage drives the design. The company knows more precisely what it is selling, what value it is creating and for whom it is creating it. #silverbullet Finding a competitive advantage is very much about taking the fate of your business into your own hands.

Related concepts to competitive advantage are uniqueness, differentiation, innovation, and superiority. We will not go any further into the definition of competitive advantage but continue to work towards finding it.

Strategic marketing skills are key

Strategic marketing is a discipline, a multidisciplinary field. For example, from the point of view of creating a new product, it is "nothing" on its own; it requires the right environment. It's like pharmacology. Once you master pharmacology, you can develop medication to treat cholesterol, a cold, or coronavirus. The same applies to strategic marketing. Mastering it enables the creation of new things.

This is how Professor Peter Doyle has described the differences between sales and marketing:

> Selling and marketing are contrasting in their approaches. Selling tries to push the customer to buy what the business has. Marketing, on the other hand, tries to get the organization to develop and offer the customer will find is of real value.

Framework for the toolkit

The framework for the Find Your Competitive Advantage toolkit™ was found in this definition of strategic marketing:

> The science and art of exploring, creating, and delivering value to satisfy the needs of a target market at a profit. Marketing identifies unfulfilled needs and desires. It defines, measures, and quantifies the size of the identified market and the profit potential. It pinpoints which segments the company is capable of serving best and it designs and promotes the appropriate products and services.
>
> *Philip Kotler, professor, author, consultant*

The definition stripped down and prepared as keywords:

Science," art" ...

...exploring, creating, delivering value...

...to satisfy the needs, target market...

...identifies unfulfilled needs and desires...

...defines, measures, quantifies, the identified market, the profit potential

...segments, capable of serving...

...and promotes the appropriate products and services

The three pillars

There are three aspects of the definition of strategic marketing that I think are worth noting:

- Strategic marketing is business-driven at the strategic level (not just at the functional level)
- It starts with creating value for the customer (no mention of beating the competition)
- Marketing communications are only at the end of the value chain.

So, what is strategic marketing in practice? How could it be explained in an understandable way? In order to understand the definition more clearly, I shortened Kotler's definition into a wireframe model:

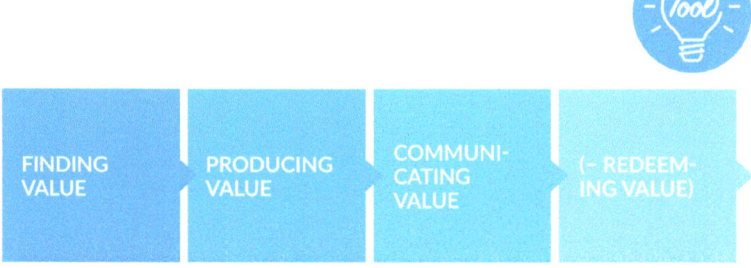

Figure 1. The stages of Kotler's value process.

The discovery of value, which is the left edge of the picture, is the direction in which this book also wants to encourage its readers to look for value that no other company has yet found. When you go there, you will end up at the source of value for the customer. There, the ocean is blue.

Finding value requires creativity (as Kotler's definition implies).

Value production, in turn, is the production of the value that was found in such a way that it can be delivered to the customer, who in turn can create value for their target group's operations. Productization, servitization, branding, a business idea, and business model development are all methods of value production in this context.

You need to assess your company's ability and resources to deliver the value you have found, as well as the economic potential of your idea. You need to identify the markets to which the value you find can be offered, and you also need to segment and define them.

Communicating value is the skill of taking the discovered and produced value to the market. First to your own organisation and selected stakeholders, and then to the awareness of the market. Without excellent communication, even the "best" product will not reach the market. It is pointless to argue that a good product sells itself. That hasn't been true since the launch of the internet.

The final stage of the value process is the redemption of the discovered and created value. The customer gets what the company's product or service promises: it helps the customer do what the customer does, it brings the promised value to the customer's operations.

The main part of our understanding of marketing has to do with the marketing on the right-hand side of the image. If you draw a dividing line down the middle of the image, you'll find that the vast majority of marketing and marketing players operate on the right-hand side of the line. That's where the skills and activities we commonly call marketing are. It also helps to explain why marketing is often perceived as advertising and marketing communications.

> **Thus, according to Kotler's definition, strategic marketing skills and marketing are two different things. There is marketing – and there are strategic *marketing skills*.**

The 4 Ps model turns into a market-oriented 4 Cs model

The 4 Ps model of marketing, familiar to many, describes the role of marketing in an organisation. It is built on product-oriented thinking. Rethinking it as market-oriented turns it the other way around into the 4 Cs model, according to Professor Don E. Schultz:

Product > **Consumer/client**

The marketer needs to understand what the customer wants and needs. It is not enough to sell what you can make yourself; instead, you have to create products and services that meet the needs of a specific target group. Creating value for the customer is a fundamental element of strategic marketing.

Price > **Cost**

For the modern consumer, the price tag on a product is only one of the factors influencing a purchase decision. For example, what does it cost to buy a product when you pick it up? And what about the environmental costs of producing, transporting, and using it? What does it mean in the longer term if the consumer eats it every day? When considered this way, the price becomes a very broad question. Let's take the example of a banana tree. For Fair Trade bananas, it is not enough that they are produced "fairly"; the whole production–logistics–sale chain must work in the same way.

Place > **Convenience**

The convenience and ease of buying a product are important. Which medium or channel would work best, what is the delivery time, and when should the product be available? For example, you can often get a book online from retailers such as Amazon more quickly than ordering from your local bookshop. The internet allows you to shop when it suits you best, 24/7.

Promotion > **Communication**

Successful communication is fundamentally about listening and understanding. Aim to create interactive communication. Move from advertising and marketing communications to more holistic communications. Don't advertise - provoke thought with communication. Actively involve the target group, stimulate debate.

Moving on to the toolkits department

It's time to move on to the so-called toolkits department. To get started, we will go through the Strategic Options section of the toolkit. Its role is to help you navigate alternative directions and the scenarios they create, from which you can seek a competitive advantage. The toolkit acts as a kind of instrument, a flight simulator, and a landscape creator to open up new ways of thinking and consider options through the eyes of an explorer. The idea is to provide perspectives that you wouldn't have thought of or looked for yourself. The police would call them lines of inquiry.

In many cases, the development of a company involves examining the industry, segments, and categories. Considering the solutions of competitors. Taking out a spreadsheet and creating linear success models (living the pea green view of reality mentioned earlier).

Of course, you have to do all of the above as well, but you are unlikely to create a superior new thing by that method. Creating something new requires new thinking. Neither Spotify nor IKEA were born from thinking about what competitors were doing. They were based on people and human behaviour. They were social and cultural innovations. Finding and creating the idea for these and similar innovations required human sciences, business anthropology, and creativity.

Product-oriented thinking has produced some devilishly persistent paths of thinking. The strategic directions presented will broaden your thinking and break the straitjacket of product-oriented thinking. When considering strategic directions, the idea is to combine scenario work with the development of practical competitive advantage. The big, underlying idea is that an SME does not have the same opportunity (or need) to shape the future as a large company, or to consider how its development views coincide with the future. A smart company has future literacy, but the idea behind this toolkit is that the company is active: the party that creates the future (rather than standing back and watching).

Scenario work must, of course, be done. Building a vision of the future is an essential part of perceiving the landscape, of immersing oneself in the challenge. But since the future is always ahead and no one, despite all possible research, can know it for sure, it is worth taking control of the future by creating it.

Strategic directions

There are seven strategic directions. They allow not only companies but also products, services, or organizations (municipalities or other public sector operators) to sketch out scenarios to find a competitive advantage. The toolkit allows the company to choose different directions in which to simulate its alternative for a competitive advantage.

We use the term "company" here as a generic term for practical reasons: it avoids having to read the same comma-driven string of product, service, company, organisation over and over again.

To clarify, let's recap: At the beginning of the book, when we went through typical strategies such as "we want to be the market leader" or "the best in such and such a segment", the term 'strategy' referred to the goal the company wanted to achieve. Here, strategic directions aim to help the company find the factor that will help it achieve its objectives. The question is, "what is the superior means" or "what is the thing" required to achieve the goal and the means to achieve "market leadership".

SET OF TOOLKITS

Direction 1: The company creates something radical and new

In this strategic direction, the company sets out to find a new, unprecedented, market-changing competitive advantage – something big that has never even been imagined. Often, it is so radical that a competitor cannot copy or challenge it. Creating something radical and new means that a company creates something that no one else has created before. Others have not had the skills, courage, or insight to take action.

A radical thing is unparalleled and unprecedented. Something radical and new is often a solution that no one has thought of because "the market already has everything", and there are already many improved versions of the existing things.

The steam engine was a radical innovation in its time. Apple's touchscreen smartphone is a familiar example of something new and radical for its time. It was a radical idea, which was then taken up by other operators as well. Radical new things are rarely created. A radical new thing can also create new markets (and not just improve existing ones). Disruptions that challenge industries and industry boundaries are often radical innovations. The platform economy is often the basis for disruptive innovations.

> The term 'radical' is often defined as extreme, stark, revolutionary.

Direction 2: The company perceives a change in the industry – and shapes the business to fit it

Industries are constantly changing, as are the segments within them. In this strategic horizon, the company reflects on developments in its industry.

Brands are important drivers of change. Their use affects us as individuals and shapes our behaviour. As a result of digitalisation, disruptive solutions have challenged even large players. MobilePay introduced a new way to pay and transfer money between persons and businesses. As a result, institutional banks have been forced to follow its lead.

From megatrends (climate change with its many consequences, immigration, populism, population growth, an increasing life expectancy, the growing importance of technology, etc.) to global competition, there are more variables than ever, either directly or indirectly. Sustainability (ESG, etc.) is already included in the branding of so many companies that it is no longer enough to be an actual competitive advantage, but it is an increasingly important competitive factor. In many industries and segments, responsible behaviour is at least a hygiene factor: it is a prerequisite for a company to be able to operate in a competitive market at all.

For example, the traditional vinyl record was replaced by the DVD, which again was overthrown as king of the hill by streaming services. It wasn't reasonable for Polaroid to stick with its photo system when a high-quality camera could be installed on a smartphone.

In many sectors, leading companies are growing larger and larger. They also often define the market supply. Because competition is global, a company that focuses on its home market also has international competitors. It is, therefore, important to understand the big changes that are affecting businesses. The logic of competition lives and changes all the time. Challenging the market leader directly is not worthwhile, but creating a business idea in "pockets left unnoticed" by the market leader can be a recipe for success. In many cases, ideas born in the pockets that the big player did not pick up have later attracted the attention and buying interest of the bigger player. This is what happened when Facebook bought WhatsApp.

Here are a few more options for different roles that show how a company can adapt to change and seek a competitive advantage:

Toolkit

A challenger tries to complement with its own offering what the bigger player has not been able or willing to take into account. Finding a competitive advantage requires interaction with current and potential customers to gather relevant information for the challenger to further find a competitive advantage.

A copycat uses the competence developed by others. It offers a product that someone else has already made familiar. A copycat walks the trail made by someone else but with its own solution.

A specialist takes advantage of needs that others have overlooked. This can be specialisation in serving a particular segment or specialisation in a particular skill. The idea is the same as focusing. A specialist can also act as a partner to a larger player: it operates in a symbiotic relationship where both benefit from each other.

Direction 3: The company creates something incrementally new

Creating something incrementally new means improving on what already exists or creating something new that offers something better than the alternatives already on the market. In this scenario, the company perceives the patterns of the industry and tries to create something that brings something new to the market. Whatever that "something" is, it must contain something new and relevant, specifically from the customer's point of view. It is not enough for it to be relevant in the eyes of the company producing it.

There are clear differences between radical and incremental competitive advantages; where radical is something that has not been thought of before, incremental is development on a smaller scale. One could say that when there is plenty of supply in a particular industry and the options are largely similar in the eyes of customers, even a small improvement, and thus differentiation for the better, can be a decisive step forward.

> The dictionary definition of 'incremental' is gradually increasing and slightly more developed.

Direction 4: The company recreates itself

This is where we go back to square one, so to speak.

In this scenario, the company is already in operation. Business operations may have been profitable, but changes in the business environment are visible or have already created cracks in the windscreen. Or perhaps the company recognises that competence needs to be developed further to ensure success. The company may have experienced scenario 2 (perceived changes in the industry). There are many companies that have lost their market position for reasons such as the burgeoning Chinese market.

"We have the skills, we know the market and its logic, our machinery is in good condition, our staff is competent. But how do we recreate ourselves?" is the key question.

Rather than dwelling on the past, it is worth taking up the definition of strategic marketing and shifting the focus from product and price orientation to market orientation. This may also redefine the market in which the company operates. Redefining your market also helps you to see new perspectives. For example, Unikulma (page xx) has been doing this for decades and has evolved from a bed retailer to a sleep specialist.

It is worth considering whether a product-driven company could recreate itself by refining the value of its products and increasing the proportion of services in its offering. This was done with great success by the Finnish surface material manufacturer PuuComp (page xx)

A company operating in this strategic direction turns its focus from product portfolios or price-driven thinking to customer needs.

Direction 5: Focusing

In this option, the company focuses on doing something in a particular area of expertise, or it focuses on the specific needs of an often narrow target group. This may be because the bigger players are unwilling or unable to take over a particular segment. Or competitors have not understood the needs of the target group. Finding competitive advantage through focus requires differentiation.

Price competition is also a form of focusing, but we will not comment on it here.

Direction 6: **Market shaping**

This strategic direction as a concept encompasses a wide range of different concepts and solutions, which can be called market shaping. The Uber ride-hailing service and Airbnb accommodation service are familiar ideas and business models. Spotify is a familiar example of market shaping. Its founders brought together on a single platform all the players in the music business, including musicians, composers, concert and gig promoters, bands, lyrics writers and producers – the whole range of professionals and companies already in the business. They created a new idea of an ecosystem that now serves as a common platform for all.

As this book is primarily aimed at sole entrepreneurs, micro companies, and small and medium-sized enterprises, we use a smaller scale for the description. Market shaping is the search for a new idea among an existing set of players. It does not have to take years to develop or require huge loans in the start-up phase. In market shaping, all players involved work in a new way through the idea and business model. The basic idea behind market shaping is to create new offerings and new ways of doing things, just as SuperSon, presented in the company examples, has done.

Direction 7: **Business as usual**

This is also an option. Even staying in place in a hyper-competitive environment requires development and renewal. Many companies have tried efficiency measures, and the cheese slicer has already been used more than once. As toolkits, they work up to a point, but without digging out the customer perspective and refining the business idea around it, it is difficult to find the ingredients for growth. When markets change with the changing supply, customers' expectations are reshaped; the company's familiar and secure relative position on the star chart of businesses changes because the stars on the chart change places.

This option can also be compared to a mould problem. You can cover a mouldy area with a layer of paint, but the mould spores will still tend to multiply. Mould may be out of sight for a while, but over time it becomes a bigger problem.

There is an old saying that when things are going well, you should start thinking about the next step. In a competitive market, success is only success for the time being. Even a successful concept will eventually come to an end.

Of course, there may also be legitimate reasons for continuing in the old way. It is possible that there are a lot of drivers in the operation that have been used to stabilize the operation at a steady state, at the desired cruising altitude. It could be that the company already has a competitive advantage that has allowed it to earn a solid position in the market. If the situation of the company is so favourable, it is probably worthwhile to work out the elements of competence that can be used to further develop it.

Three different competitive advantages

We have just navigated through seven different landscapes and evaluated the main options they offer. Hopefully, they offered some different perspectives. Surely they generated a lot of good questions, but the initial reflections provide fewer good answers. It is, therefore, worth considering what kind of competitive advantage companies are looking for. What would be the right solution for the business?

Professor Michael E. Porter talks a lot about a permanent competitive advantage, "eternal and set in stone". In today's ruthless and hyper-competitive environment, a permanent competitive advantage is probably a utopia. There will always be a challenger, a new king of the hill. As this book and this toolkit are aimed at businesses and want to encourage the discovery of competitive advantage, it is time to define competitive advantage at different levels. The keys to this were found in the companies analysed for the toolkit. We found three different competitive advantages, which are

- strategic competitive advantage
- decisive competitive advantage
- differentiating competitive advantage.

Classifying competitive advantages into three categories also helps and inspires the search and discovery of a competitive edge. In the classical sense, we generally talk about strategic competitive advantage. It often refers to a superior competitive advantage that cannot be challenged by the company's competitors. It is the foundation on which the strategy is built, guaranteeing the company a stable and solid position in the market. Tesco can be said to have a strategic competitive advantage, symbolised and driven by Tesco Clubcard Pay+. It is the result of a long and consistent effort. But even that alone will not dominate the market. Tesco also faces competition both as a group and at the level of the companies it owns.

Nokia's mobile phones had a competitive advantage, but as we all know, the company lost its position because it was unable to adapt to changes in the environment, such as the needs of application developers. Apple came along and reshaped the market.

Here are three different types of competitive advantage, with definitions:

Toolkit: Strategic competitive advantage

Strategic competitive advantage is the most significant of the competitive advantages. It is born when a company creates something radically new. The kind of thing you didn't expect, or the kind of thing no one else is able to do – at least profitably. The strategic competitive advantage is generated by strategic policy number 1.

Strategic competitive advantage is not within reach of every company, as the examples later in this book will show. Strategic competitive advantage and the resulting business idea may be such a radical innovation that it can be challenging to take to market (as the Noccela case on page xx shows) because it represents something that has not been imagined or expected. Strategic competitive advantage is a revolutionary solution.

It is clear that "we don't need that" or "how come" reactions can be met with resistance – or they can be difficult to perceive.
Synonyms for the strategic definition in this context:
important, significant, radical

Toolkit: Decisive competitive advantage

When a competitive advantage is decisive, it by definition leads to a solution or is a game changer or significant. All these are clear and heavy terms. When a competitive advantage is decisive, it is also a game changer. It adds something new to an existing supply or creates something new in itself. Where a strategic competitive advantage cannot be reached or duplicated by everyone, a decisive competitive advantage is within reach of any company. The vast majority of the company examples in this book can be categorised as having a decisive competitive advantage.

Competitive advantage, as we said, has two functions. It either allows you to do something better or saves the customer money. While a strategic competitive advantage is revolutionary, a decisive competitive advantage is evolutionary.

Radical competitive advantages and decisive competitive advantages are also primarily "reason-based" solutions (while, of course, there may also be emotional factors behind the choice).

Toolkit: **Differentiating competitive advantage**

A differentiating competitive advantage is an opportunity to find a competitive advantage, created by the modern, media-driven environment. The many, often similar, offerings are made visible through active communication, thanks to things such as social media, where different tribes, groups, and news circles have emerged. Social capital is an important driving force in creating this competitive advantage. Active and consistent investment in communication can make a company stand out in a positive way, even if the product or service itself is similar to that of its competitors.

With media hype and market volume on the rise, making constant noise is not to gain a competitive advantage. The media presentations must have a plot and a concept to ensure consistency. When it comes to a person representing the company, they must also have charisma and personality. It's not enough to criticise your competitors; you need to have content that brings something new to your target audiences – and challenges existing solutions on the market. Often, a differentiating competitive advantage is built on the personality of the person representing the company (this is close to building a personal brand).

It should be noted that the definition of differentiating competitive advantage is not fully in line with the market-oriented philosophy of this book. This book encourages you to build a competitive advantage based on customer needs and value – just as represented by strategic competitive advantage and decisive competitive advantage. Differentiating competitive advantage is based on differentiation from competitors, which is fundamentally a product-based competitive advantage.

Differentiating competitive advantage can be based on things such as the brand image. "This company sells homes in the same way as its competitors, but I have a feeling that the company I've chosen is the best option for selling my home," someone might say to justify their decision.

Social capital and its management are important competences in this option. Neliöt Liikkuu, described in the Company Cases section, is a company that has been able to take advantage of the opportunities offered by social media while challenging traditional players with its messages.

Starting points for creating a competitive advantage

It is also useful to identify the starting points (internal or external) from which the company is seeking and further redeeming its competitive advantage. The timing of the change will also affect resource decisions. As we said, radical competitive advantage is not for all companies. A start-up, an existing business, or a business that is just starting up has certain resources at its disposal, namely knowledge capital, which consists of human capital, structural capital, and relational capital. In the search for competitive advantage, resources, conditions, and objectives must be balanced and/or have a realistic relationship. Goals and conditions must interact. Here are a few starting points to help you think about the balance between resources and goals:

A company can set out to find a competitive advantage
in the following ways:

1. goal-oriented

2. market-oriented

3. resource-oriented.

Toolkit: Goal-oriented

For example, a company can find a potential direction in the market through actions like sharpening and developing its service offering. Market forecasting is one way of assessing changes. The environment may also have changed, which may force a company to reposition itself, as shown in the following example:

"The market has changed. In the longer term, we need to strategically position ourselves to offer a more holistic service to our customers."

A critical assessment must, therefore, be made of the efforts needed to achieve the goal. Do we already have the necessary competence? Should we stop providing certain services? Does the culture support servitization? What opportunities does our brand offer to capture it? Is it economically viable? What do we give up in order to prioritize our resources properly?

Toolkit: Market-oriented

The company realises that there is a need in the market for a certain kind of competence that no one else has noticed. The radar shows that there is a white spot, a need and a space for innovation in the market. The company has found value and sets out to create a new product. This option is about creating a new segment:

"We have identified a need in the market that none of our competitors has yet observed. We will try to capture it as soon as possible."

What are the conditions for the commercialization and capture of value? Do products or services need to be removed from our portfolio to secure the necessary investments?

Do we have enough social capital in-house, or do we need to recruit? Does our approach lend itself to creating value? How does this affect our brand image?

A good way of outlining a company's product portfolio and considering its internal priorities is to use the Boston Consulting Group's toolkit, a brief introduction to which can be found on page xxx.

Toolkit: Resource-oriented

When it comes to seeking a competitive advantage, the decision can be made to base it on the competence of your team (and possible network):

"We have this team, these resources and this competence. How do we develop a competitive advantage with the skills we already have?"

What information do we have about our customers? Where have we succeeded? How should we segment our customer base? Do we need to create a new culture? Are silos an obstacle? How should we involve marketing, communication, ICT, R&D and HR in the development?

Resource-oriented business development is discussed in more detail on page xx. Resource-based competitive advantage development is an excellent starting point for public administrations.

Toolkit: Assess the degree of urgency

There are many questions under each option. They are always case-specific, and there are no ready-made solutions. The company is also justified in considering its resources in relation to the urgency of the change. The need for change can be divided into three levels of urgency:

- The change has been noticed, but there is still no burning rush.
- Change is already having a visible impact, and we need to start developing something new.
- Change is at the top of the agenda, and there is already a burning rush to take action.

When assessing the level of urgency, it is good to start early. Even if it feels like there is no rush yet, it is good to be aware that finding a competitive advantage is the result of creative work. Identifying the problem and finding a solution requires creative work, thinking, and creative solutions. To do this successfully, we need to involve the subconscious in reflection and deliberation. Intensive cooperation between the two hemispheres of the brain. There is no fast track from identifying a problem or opportunity to finding a solution. You can read about the role of creative thinking on page xx.

Let me remind you once again of an essential point: keep your eye on the ball, i.e., finding value for the customer. It's easy to settle for a product-driven approach to reshaping your business. It feels like the easier, more familiar route to getting things moving and done.

This difference is like the difference between a wedding and a funeral. This is how we could describe the differences between product-oriented and market-oriented thinking. Working from a product perspective, strategy work is defined by segments, industries, and competitors. We collect data. We draw economic forecasting models and justify the future by time series. We consider market shares. We collect more data. It feels like the right things are being done. As we have been taught and as we are used to doing. There is a wealth of information available. The end result is often the same data that is available to the company and its competitors.

In market-oriented thinking, the idea of competitive advantage is more complex. There are three levels of innovation:

- innovations related to the company's products and services
- innovations related to markets and consumer behaviour
- innovations related to the company's culture and ways of working

Data as such does not create anything new, but it should be used to create insights. Insights should be market-based, market-oriented. Our toolkits are business anthropology and human sciences.

Also make use of classic toolkits

To broaden your thinking, it may also be worth introducing the most appropriate strategy toolkits presented on page xxx, many of which are already familiar to you. These include the PESTEL Analysis, VRIO Framework and BCG Matrix. The groupings of toolkits show that only a few are fundamentally focused on creating something new. As all the toolkits have been in use for a long time, we will take a cursory glance at them on page xx. The toolkits, which are categorised under the headings Toolkits for creating something new and Toolkits for developing resources, are discussed in more detail in the chapter Expanding thinking on page xxx.

Toolkit: Positioning to see near and far

The scope of the search for competitive advantage can range from far-reaching scenarios to a specific customer segment in a single industry and its individual needs. This can be done by drawing arcs from the present to the future and from history to the present day – in search of a possible next stage. The closer you get to a particular segment, the more you can justify digging out a positioning toolkit from the toolkit (which will not be presented here). By landing on the ground from a so-called drone view using a positioning toolkit, a company can analyse the position of an idea in a given segment and among competing players and brands in that segment.

A good positioning toolkit takes stock of the market situation not only from the perspective of the target audience but also from the perspective of the competition. Competition between companies always takes place within a segment and in the minds of customers. We should remember that a brand is built in the minds of the customers and through their experiences. The company can only try to guide this.

From a market perspective, finding the right segment (see the definition of strategic marketing) and analysing it is more important than looking at the industry. What is its potential? What is the company's ability to create value for it? Segment analysis is also important because it allows the company to assess the competitors and their brands operating in the segment. Issues to be addressed include:

- Are there leading brands among the competitors?
- How do they react to newcomers?
- What is the future and potential of the segment?
- What is the company's position in the minds of your target group compared to the competitors?

Segment-specific analysis provides a more accurate and fruitful overview than an analysis of the industry. This brings us closer to the needs and potential of the target group.

Segmentation helps you to be more perceptive and sensitive than a simple industry analysis. It is a key step in the process of finding and creating value. Segmentation is also the basis for impactful communication.

FINDING A COMPETITIVE ADVANTAGE IN THE COMPANY'S RESOURCES

This chapter looks for a competitive advantage in the company's resources. The competitive advantage can apply to the whole company, or it can be created on the basis of specific competence or services. Competitive advantage may lie in a company's strengths, processes, networks, and/or ways of working. This is called the resource-based approach to competitive advantage. Compared to a physical product and its competitive advantage, we are now discussing more abstract things and relying on intangible capital.

The success of a business is always a reflection of doing things successfully for customers. The company may have done well financially year after year. The need to seek a competitive advantage has perhaps not been seen for this reason. Or perhaps the competitive advantage has been created by doing, but it has not been recognised as a competitive advantage. Perhaps the company has been a particularly good partner for customers in a particular area, with a particular service or product. A good financial result may be explained by the fact that the sector has grown. The tide lifts all boats.

A successful company often adds services or products to its menu because a competitor is doing the same. "The more products, the better." The company may think that new services will bring new customers and new turnover. At the same time, it may lose its grip on the competence that is essential for success. A competitive company may lose focus.

© Vierula Consulting 2024
M. Vierula, *Find Your Market-Oriented Competitive Advantage*,
https://doi.org/10.1007/978-3-031-71663-8_6

From competitiveness to competitive advantage

Competitiveness, in the context of business, refers to the internal and external factors that enable a company to succeed in free competition. Competitors, price, location, accessibility, products, the resources available in the company, and so on are all elements of competitiveness. Competitiveness is the foundation on which a company can build a competitive advantage.

Competitor and business environment analyses and different scenarios for the future are naturally an essential part of the search for competitive advantage. However, it is worth pointing out once again that, in the context of this book, differentiation from the competition is not the factor on which competitive advantage is built. It is wise to know what your competitors are doing, but the value for a creating competitive advantage must be found in the factors that are valuable to your customers.

Customer satisfaction surveys and tacit feedback are a good starting point for exploring this in more depth. Customer segmentation helps analyse which group of customers has repeatedly given good feedback on the company's performance. What about the performance has been successful – from the customer's point of view? Companies should consider what kind of competence they have within the organisation. Where do people feel successful? What parts of interaction have led customers to praise the company or express their satisfaction? And what do the staff think is the best area of competence in the company?

Scrutinizing failures

As important as it is to look for and analyse successes, it is also important to pay attention to failures. It is good to find out why the company failed. It is wise to reflect further on what the failure meant for the customer. Do we even know how significant the failure was for the customer? Was the company missing a resource? Can you build a competitive advantage on this?

Competitive advantage through a product or service

If a company offers a wide range of services to its customers, it may make sense to look for competitive advantage through a specific service or customer segment rather than at the level of the organisation as a whole.

A company operating in several sectors may have several very different target groups. This is the case, for example, for a shipping company with both cruise and cargo customers. Or a company whose expertise is in cars may have two different segments: for some, it provides day-to-day service station services, and for others, workshop services. The needs of these segments are not the same.

In line with market-oriented thinking, competitive advantage can be sought from the needs of individual segments. Of course, the company's overall image and reputation must be in good shape, but the value must be distilled to meet the needs of a specific segment. So, there are two fronts: the development of the company's overall image and the needs of a specific segment. A monolithic, single-brand solution does not always have enough depth.

An accountancy firm that offers more than one service can start by looking at which of its services have been praised by clients. Is it perhaps payroll? Or perhaps accounting services that support management-level decision-making? Or tax counselling?

While seeking a competitive advantage, it is worth doing scenario work and analysing the future long-term relevance of industries and services by asking questions such as: In which segment is growth expected? Where are the industry and this specific segment heading? Where will we excel in the future? How is our industry changing?

Scenarios help to get an idea of the landscape ahead, but the scenarios created and the variables they contain are usually the same for all companies. "General knowledge does not provide a competitive advantage," points out Professor of Practice **Nando Malmelin**. There is plenty of data to back up scenario work, but it is more important to process the large amount of data into further insights for further development – and from that, further refine quality, better solutions for customers' daily lives.

If a company operates in, say, three different sectors where all buyers and customers have different needs, a monolithic approach is not optimal for understanding customer needs, processes, expectations, and operations. Every sector needs to go to the source of customer value to ensure that it is found.

One key idea behind the definition of strategic marketing was that a company must have the capacity to develop a product and deliver on its promise. Therefore, analysing the knowledge capital within the company and harmonising it to pursue different future directions is a key part of the search for competitive advantage. To get a full picture of the situation, you will need two pairs of glasses: one to see far away, the other to see close up.

It's also good to remember that a company doesn't have to scratch its head over possible future directions. There is nothing to stop a company from deciding for itself what its future will be like. Breakthroughs often happen when you swim against the current and make a conscious effort to avoid what everyone else (your competitors) is likely to do. When you go where the others go, you will find yourself in the middle of the pack – in the throes of price competition in the red sea.

Core capabilities and core competences

A successful business always has successes behind it. It might be difficult to discern what the ingredients for success are. Success factors can be found in processes, network management, product/service combinations, or culture. By success factors, Tero Vuorinen, DEconSc, refers to core capabilities, core competences and finding the "resource bundle".

Core competences are skills related to a specific part of the value chain, such as payroll or tax law or, for instance in the case of a law firm, dispute resolution. Core capabilities are the ability to manage the value chain as a whole, for instance so that a firm providing tax law services creates a competitive advantage from its core competence in a way that serves the client in a holistic way. A resource bundle is the set of skills within a company that that service is shaped around to ensure a competitive advantage.

In the case of a law firm or accountancy firm, certain services are fundamentally very generic and operational in nature. Payroll, for example, is repetitive and regular. Regardless of the service provider, the end result is always the same payroll calculations. From the customer's point of view, the crucial difference may be the customer experience.

Tax planning and management-level accounting services may have a different value to the client than, say, payroll. They are consultative in nature; the relationship is more partner-like, and the outcome of the work is always the result of interaction through specific expertise. In this way, the services provide more value to the client company's management than payroll.

The ingredients of attitude?

An accounting firm may find a competitive advantage for management-level accounting services in the form of things like emotional factors. If clients have praised an accountancy firm for its "attitude" in handling matters, this may be a source of competitive advantage if it is a valuable skill for clients. What has it taken to create and implement this "attitude", and what are its ingredients? Why has the "attitude" been praised? What is its role in what the customer does?

You need to be able to analyze and see the components of the resource bundle. If a company adopts the "attitude" praised by customers as its competitive advantage, this must be raised as a policy to be collectively refined; the attitude must be carried through at all stages. In this context, we could talk about competence design. The term is not in common use, so here is a brief explanation of its meaning in this context.

Competence design

Competence design is about discovering the elements that the customer has found valuable. They may be parts of a process or a certain attitude toward doing things. The idea behind competence design is to unravel these elements and reassemble them into a value-creating process. These critical elements are then further refined into an interaction. The competence identified as excellent will be further refined into a harmonious whole. This can also be called synthesis. So, it is not enough for a company to have an "attitude"; it is also necessary to create a process for recreating this attitude time and time again to ensure consistency at all points of contact.

'Orchestration' could be a handy term to describe competence design. In this case, the company creates a composition for a particular skill that provides value to the customer. Not only is each individual instrument outstanding, but the orchestra is also a highly tuned ensemble. This creates refined competence capital.

It is the competence capital within a company that gives it a competitive advantage. It must be possible to assess whether the policy has the potential for continuity and contains the necessary criteria for success also in the future. The core competencies of owners and key personnel, assessments of industry trends, and informed views on customer preferences are dimensions to be outlined.

Strategy is about deciding what a company will do – and what it will not do. It is not possible to formulate all of a company's services as a competitive advantage. It is up to the management and owners of the company to make a policy on what the strategic services are – both in the shorter and longer term.

 Developing customer-oriented thinking and processes is a form of slash-and-burn agriculture. The soil is burnt so that it can be more fertile after a while.

Practising the pattern game

In a relay race, a lot of practice is given to changing the baton. In training, they practice at what point the baton is passed to the next runner, how the receiver's hand is extended, how the baton is handed over, and what grip is used to receive it. In football, for example, you practise playing the ball away from your own area in a small space in two-on-three situations and develop different patterns for free kicks, which you then practise as a team. Individual playing positions are also taught. Similar approaches are used to process a bundle of resources into a value chain. It is, therefore, also about developing team play. Placed on the strategic marketing wireframe model, in developing a resource bundle, we move in the space between value discovery and value creation.

In a resource-oriented search for competitive advantage, the details must be taken care of in a way that is appropriate for the whole. We need to distil a value chain on which we can create a competitive edge. Often, this means breaking down silos and creating a new way of working.

The core idea behind strategic marketing competence is to transfer customer insights and perspectives to strategic decision-making for further refinement. Their role is to represent the voice of the customer in the company. The customer-oriented perspectives (needs, expectations, perceptions, etc.) familiar from business life are also applicable to public administration. On the public administration side, the traditional way of proceeding through components requires a new, more fluid way of doing things. In the search for competitive advantage, customer focus must be the starting point.

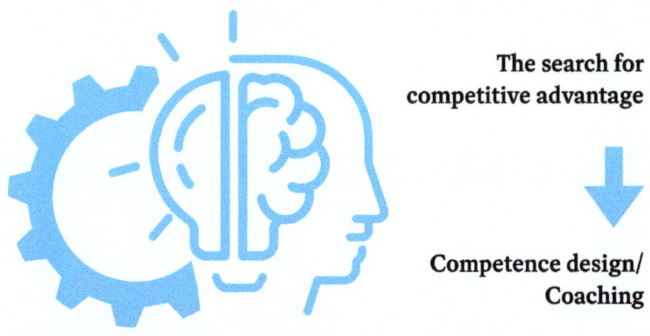

Figure 2. Competitive advantage can be found and refined from the resources available within the company.

Competitiveness already exists

 It's worth looking for lost keys in a wider area than just around the streetlamp.

The three-stage learning process

Development and evolution involve learning. The learning process can be seen as a three-stage process:

1. Learning to see what doesn't work.

2. Seeing the areas that work and are worth investing in.

3. Learning to use what you have learned and developing further.

Toolkit: Six steps in the search for a resource-based competitive advantage

The search for and implementation of a resource-based competitive advantage can be divided into six steps:

1. **Identify your organisation's resources.**
2. **Identify your own core competences and capabilities.**
3. **Assess the potential of resources and capabilities to create a competitive advantage.**
4. **Find the competitive advantage that best utilises your company's resources and capabilities in relation to the opportunities in the environment.**
5. **Identify resource gaps and complete, add to, and update your company's resource base.**
6. **Design your competence and turn resources into a competitive advantage.**

*(Source: **Tero Vuorinen**, DEconSc, adapted by Markku Vierula)*

The starting point for the search for a resource-based competitive advantage can be the perspective of a specific segment: in the case of an accountancy firm, the perspective of strategically important service buyers. This is based on an understanding of the customer's processes and what is valuable to the customer for their own success. The search for competitive advantage is creative work. Due to the specific nature of creative work, the above steps overlap in some cases.

Those seeking a competitive advantage, whether in an accountancy firm, a law firm or even a café, must first and foremost see things through the eyes of the customer. This requires an understanding of what the client is doing and what is important to them in their own activities.

Start from customer needs

Development often starts from a production- and management-oriented approach within the structures of the organisation: from the inside out. When working from the inside out, the internal objectives and strategies of functions frame the development work. Functions are often structured around production and management. Instead, development should move from the needs of customers to the resources of the organisation: from the outside in. We need to move from product thinking to service thinking. We need to be able to turn our own product and silo-based approach into a customer segment-based approach, where all encounters create value for our core customer base through consistent and collaborative work. Staff plays a key role in this.

Resources as such are no guarantee of finding a competitive advantage. We must be able to utilise our core capabilities, core competence, and resources by transforming them into a unique and superior offering. In this way, the competence of a competitive player becomes a competitive advantage.

It is, therefore, about the competence capital of the organisation and the development of individual skills into the collective competence of the organisation. Often, this also requires innovative solutions – solutions that no one else has been able to provide. Increasingly, the value of a company is made up of intangible elements. This is particularly important in the era of knowledge work and networks. For more on developing collective organisational competences, see Competitive advantage as a driver of organisational development on page 107.

Toolkit: Six steps to finding your competitive advantage

1. Make the decision to seek a competitive advantage (which requires financial and moral support from management).
2. Make the decision to have perseverance and determination.
3. Gather views from your personnel and customers.
4. Go through the scenarios provided by the toolkits and have intensive discussions both at a rational level and using creative thinking. Reflect together on whether your goal is a radical, differentiating, or decisive competitive advantage.
5. Good luck and strength in your efforts! As has been said: finding a competitive advantage is not easy.
6. Great! You can see a competitive advantage start to emerge.

As I have mentioned: creating something new from existing resources requires the ability to move around abstract issues. The key is not primarily to shape the image of the company, but to be able to bring a customer perspective into the reflection and decision-making process. Professor of Marketing Hannu Saarijärvi has said:

"The theories and concepts of marketing are broadly applicable to different sectors of society and are not limited to the business environment."

Toolkit: Five criteria for a competitive advantage

In the search for a competitive advantage, several ideas can emerge. What is the potential of a single competitive advantage idea? Its vitality can be measured against these five criteria:

1. Thoroughly deliberated and so clearly described that it offers something essentially new: either radical new, incremental new, or a differentiating competitive advantage.
2. The idea is so powerful that it feels wild even to yourself. It arouses disbelief and enthusiasm.
3. The resources are there – or can be found – to make it happen.
4. A new culture can be created based on the new competitive advantage
5. The competitive advantage can be communicated to the market.

These criteria cover the stages of the wireframe model on strategic marketing: discovering value – creating value – communicating value. If you can proudly tick 5 x ✓ of the criteria, that's great. When a radical or incremental idea is refined, you are creating something new and superior. Once a company has come this far, it is time to consider protecting and registering the Competitive Edge™.

Encoded in the competitive advantage chromosomes is the idea that competitive advantage and its resulting operating model must create value for the customer. So, it's not a bad idea to also ask customers for their opinions and views along the way. But be sure to avoid ideas scraped from the bottom of the cliché bucket. There are too many of them. The world does not need more.

When asking for opinions and carrying out A/B tests, it is also worth remembering that a radical innovation may be rejected simply because it has never been done before. Opposition can have its own message. Maybe that's what the world needs, so belief in your cause is an important driver.

 A market-oriented company is innovative by definition because it strives to exceed expectations.

CONCRETE BUSINESS EXAMPLES

I have now gone through the Find Your Competitive Advantage™ toolkit or, more precisely, the toolkit. The book has so far described a number of strategic directions that can be used to map out and navigate competitive situations and changes. This book has introduced a "flight simulator" that has given new perspectives on making sense of the horizon. I have said that the ingredients may be present in the competence and resources of your company.

The toolkit is modelled on examples from excellent companies, as I described earlier. We are now looking at companies of different types and sizes. All the companies used as "material" for this toolkit have an exemplary competitive advantage and business idea. Each one has an interesting, superior element that makes it easy to form an elevator pitch.

In the company introductions, I will briefly describe their activities and business idea and assess which of the seven strategic options the business idea represents. I will also define the competitive advantage of each company.

For certain companies, we also highlight the role of communication, as without excellent communication, even the best idea does not exist.

My educated guess is that the competitive advantages of the companies have not in all cases been developed consistently. Rather, they have been the result of passionate entrepreneurial activity and have developed in everyday life or have otherwise simply matured favourably.

The descriptions do not focus on performance, but only on competitive advantages and business ideas. All the companies selected have "their thing": something that makes them different from their competitors or makes them appeal to their target group, or something that immediately stood out clearly. In addition to their competitive advantage, some companies have other elements in their business model that they want to bring to their industry.

The businesses are grouped into two main categories: business to business and business to consumer. It is worth noting that some companies operate in both sectors.

© Vierula Consulting 2024
M. Vierula, *Find Your Market-Oriented Competitive Advantage*,
https://doi.org/10.1007/978-3-031-71663-8_7

Some companies have a great name that describes their business area. These have been translated into English to help you, the reader, understand the business idea better. A carefully chosen name is often an integral part of a company's brand.

Even if your own business is active in, say, the consumer market, it is also worth looking at B2B examples. Good ideas know no boundaries, so there may be inspiring concepts for developing your activities on the other side of the fence.

So, let's put the competitive advantages and business ideas in the spotlight!

B2C examples

Knitting grannies at the heart of Myssyfarmi

Myssyfarmi (Knit Farm) is a farm-based design business.

The company's business idea is to hand-knit individual wool hats and other accessories such as scarves, headbands, and gloves. Organic wool from Finnish sheep is used to make the products. The wool is washed and spun in contract spinning mills and hand-dyed at Myssyfarmi's production facilities.

All the products are knitted by local pensioner women, the Myssy Grannies. The purchaser or recipient of a Myssyfarmi product can check the label on the product to see which granny has knitted it. The grannies are presented in the personnel gallery on the company's website.

In autumn 2020, Myssyfarmi launched a joint outdoor clothing collection in collaboration with another rural Finnish company, Sasta. The company went international when the Parisian Galeries Lafayette department store included the Myssyfarmi X Sasta collection in its selection. The rural spirit and brand are nicely underlined by the company's slogan: It's not cool. It's warm.

> The strategic direction of Myssyfarmi is the creation of something incrementally new. It can also be seen as a creator of radical new. As a farm-based business, Myssyfarmi cooperates with other businesses in the countryside, so it has a very close-knit network of partners. The concept is well-developed in terms of production, raw material sourcing, partners, and branding.
>
> The company's competitive edge is a strategic competitive advantage, and Myssyfarmi has defined its own market. Under these conditions, it is difficult to challenge.
>
> **Myssyfarmi.fi**

Neliöt Liikkuu confused from the start

"We do not have a separate vision, mission, slogan, or value proposition. We've already summed up everything essential in our name."

The name Neliöt Liikkuu (Squares Move) sums up the philosophy of the real estate agency. This success is due, among other things, to a strong media presence led by the founder, Andrei Koivumäki. His personality is strongly linked to his company. There has been a lot of discussion in the media about both the company and its founder. The man even ended up on the cover of the high-end Image magazine. We can safely conclude that this is a phenomenon.

When the company, and Koivumäki with it, became successful, this was interpreted as part of the company's branding and public image. This broke the Finnish ideal of cultivating modesty. The idea was to challenge the "traditional" ways of doing real estate and to renew perceptions of the real estate industry. The financial results were also made public. New ways of working and fresh, clear thinking are embodied in the company's name.

"We have come to change the whole industry; we brought the appreciation and attitude that the industry has been lacking", the founders of the company declared at the start.

> The company's strategic direction is to perceive a change in the industry and bring something new to it. The company brought something incrementally new to the business environment. The competitive edge is a differentiating competitive advantage, as communication was the main focus in the early days and was deliberately publicity-seeking. The content of the communication was so industry-shaking that there were certainly some mutters about the language and ways of doing things.
>
> **Neliotliikkuu.fi**

FabPatch patches clothes

The business idea for a repair patch for textiles was born from the challenges of a family with children: worn-out socks, unravelled coat hems and holes on trouser knees. Repairing them would have required darning with a needle and thread. Or, the broken clothes could have been thrown away and/or the materials recycled. But this was not the right option for the founders of FabPatch, and they realised that clothes could be repaired with a band-aid, so to speak.

Design know-how led to a solution: a garment band-aid that can be used to patch or cover up a torn or worn-out garment. The idea has been further refined so that the band-aids can also be used to decorate clothes. Design patterns bring expressiveness and options to users.

> The strategic direction is to create something incrementally new. Garment patches already on the market needed to be ironed, sewn, heated or glued. The FabPatch owners realised that the patch + band-aid model was a better solution.
>
> A decisive competitive advantage: Traditionally, there have been many options for mending clothes, but the garment band-aid introduced a new, easy, and quick alternative. The company's philosophy also aims to extend the life of the garment. With its creative business idea, the FabPatch makes it possible in a neat and easy way.
>
> **Vaatelaastari.fi**

The Other Danish Guy gets under your skin

This company literally gets under, or on the skin of its target audience. The Other Danish Guy specialises in men's underwear. The company believes that an individual's confidence and essence are based on their underwear. The company believes that a good pair of men's underwear is one that doesn't feel like anything. You should also not pay undue attention to your underwear.

The company slogan contains a dose of philosophy: The Fundamental Layer of Confidence™.

Another theme that runs through the brand is the idea that Only three balls matter™. That third ball of concern is our planet, which the company also wants to take care of. The underwear is the first in the world to use a "comfortably" soft and lightweight Smoothshell™ fabric made from plastic waste and discarded fishing nets.

Marketing communications are also a core competence for the company's competitive advantage. The company has succeeded in creating its own tribe through its philosophy, which it maintains through its original communication style. You could criticise the communication, saying "there's no logic or sense to it", but that's the secret. The Other Danish Guy knows its audience: some like it, some don't. The company only wants to take care of the first group.

> Strategic direction: focusing on a specific "thing" and creating something new and fresh for the industry in terms of communication. In this case, we are talking about creating something incrementally new.
>
> A differentiating competitive advantage: the history of marketing includes many examples of brands where marketing thinking and marketing communication are an integral part of the brand. The Other Danish Guy is an excellent example of that expertise as a success factor.
>
> **Theotherdanishguy.fi**

Docrates – specialised in cancer

The Docrates Cancer Hospital is a private hospital in Helsinki specialising in the diagnosis, treatment, and monitoring of cancer. Getting cancer is a serious matter, and it also affects the patient's loved ones. At Docrates Cancer Hospital, you can have immediate access to tests and treatments without a referral. Patients are treated by top cancer doctors. The patient is assigned a personal nurse. The hospital's facilities and equipment are state-of-the-art. The business model also includes the latest medicines and researched treatments. Docrates Cancer Hospital also offers its services to foreign patients.

> Strategic direction: focusing on cancer prevention and treatment through creating something radical new.
>
> This is a case of a radical competitive advantage driven by the creation of a new industry. Docrates offers a radical new solution for the client or patient and their family and friends. Of course, another player may start with the same business idea, but Docrates has a head start. The new player will need to create at least an incremental competitive advantage.
>
> **Docrates.com**

Lovia's brand value lies in its philosophy

Lovia designs and sells designer accessories. The business idea is to design and manufacture design products from materials found to be surplus and waste. Unlike with many other brands, for Lovia users, value is not created by communicating an image to others but by the philosophy behind the product.

The business model: Lovia's founders wanted to turn the design process upside down. Lovia's design products are based on materials that are usually left over from the manufacture of various products. These materials include fish skins and surplus leather from upholstering leather sofas. Transparency is also at the heart of the company's philosophy. Anyone who buys a Lovia product has access to a code that allows the buyer to see how much the person who sewed the bag was paid, where the buttons were purchased, and so on. Transparency is sought in all activities.

The company's founders are design and fashion professionals who want to resist overconsumption and draw attention to materials that already exist. "To us, there is no rubbish. There are only abandoned resources that are no longer valued," say the founders of the company about their philosophy.

"Instead of trends, materials dictate what we design. We aim to give new life to discarded materials that deserve to be loved for a long time to come."

Strategic direction: the company creates something incrementally new for the industry. Design can be enjoyed with a clear conscience and a good mind.

A decisive competitive advantage: the professional background of the founders provides a solid basis for developing the business.

Loviacollection.com

Rekki recycles well-loved brand products

Rekki (Rack) recycles women's, men's and children's clothes, shoes, and accessories through its online shop. The products on offer are from brand houses and well-known brands such as Boss, Zara, Diesel, Makia, Marimekko, Ril's, Michael Kors, Sand, and so on. Part of the business model is that the accessories put on sale are clean and do not have a strong smell. In addition, the clothes are in line with current fashion and the season. The products being sold are recycled, and all the customer has to do is send their products to Rekki. The company sorts them into clothes for sale – or for charity. So, you can donate your clothes to Rekki or sell them using your own sales account.

Rekki has a clear recycling mission. Research has shown that some clothes may only be used 7 to 10 times. For example, one-third of the clothes in Finns' wardrobes have been unused for more than a year. There is more than €2 billion worth of clothing and accessories that are no longer needed but can still be used.

The website is built around a customer-centric approach with men's, women's and children's sections, as well as outlet, clearance, and inspiration sections. The selection also includes design, party, winter, summer, edgy, premium, and smart casual themes to help make shopping easier. A blog also provides inspirational tips for dressing up.

> Strategic direction: Rekki has created something incrementally new and welcome for the industry. It encourages the recycling of little-used but modern good-quality clothes. Rekki is also looking to expand into the European market.
>
> A decisive competitive advantage: Brand products and recycling play well together from a customer perspective.
>
>
>
> **Rekki.fi**

Relove – online shop, café and recycler of premium brand products

Relove is a synthesis of a café, online shop, wine bar, and the recycling of premium and luxury brand products. Its business idea is to be a café and wine bar, second-hand shop, online shop, and/or event venue.

Relove's business model can be examined from the perspective of multiple needs. With Relove's selection, you can update your outfit collection with a recycled brand product, for example. In the café, you can enjoy an organic coffee, a pastry, or a glass of wine. The company also has second-hand racks for high-quality clothes. Relove is also a pop-up shop where partners can showcase their products and services for a predetermined period of time. Customers can also put their clothes up for sale in Relove's online shop.

Relove has two stores in Helsinki. In spring 2021, Relove opened a store at the leading Finnish high-end department store Stockmann.

> The strategic direction is a combination of perceiving an industry change and creating something incrementally new for the industry. It is interesting to try to determine whether the business is a café / wine bar, an online shop, or a clothing recycling business – or, after all, a combination of these.
>
> A decisive competitive advantage: The coffee and café market has grown dramatically in recent years. Recycling has become an increasingly important way of doing business as environmental awareness has grown. Brands are still valued. Relove as a name reflects these trends in a great way.
>
> **Relove.fi**

Restaurant Nolla – a greener dining experience

The business idea behind Restaurant Nolla (Zero) in Helsinki is to offer tasty and inventive food based on the values of sustainable development and circular economy.

In its business model, Nolla aims to take into account the smallest details. The raw materials come mainly from organic producers in the surrounding area. The company has in its restaurant a compost bin where organic waste is composted. When a food producer delivers ingredients to the restaurant, they take the contents of the compost and reuse it for their own purposes. The cutlery is all different because "there are already enough knives, forks, and spoons in the world". Cream cheese is served on the bottoms of cut wine bottles. The menu is deliberately short, as this helps to reduce food waste. Zero waste, as the restaurant's slogan says.

Only beverages produced in accordance with sustainable principles are served at Nolla. The restaurant has its own microbrewery. The company is constantly evaluating its operations in an effort to make its practices more sustainable.

Strategic direction: the aim is to create something incrementally new in the industry.

A decisive competitive advantage: minimising waste, local ingredients and producers, and the dining experience coming together.

Restaurantnolla.com

Fiksuruoka.fi helps save money and reduce food waste

Fiksu Ruoka Oy (Smart Food) is an online grocery store. The company's product range is mainly made up of clearance food items that would otherwise be at risk of being discarded. The products are the same as those sold in grocery stores.

The company promises that customers will save between 20 and 90 per cent on their grocery shopping when they use the Fiksuruoka.fi service. The company's mission also includes a promise to work with its customers to reduce food waste in Finland. An additional incentive to buy are the so-called one-cent products. So, whenever the one-cent products campaign is running, during the checkout process, shoppers can choose from a changing selection a product that costs just one cent.

The company delivers orders within 2–4 working days to destinations throughout Finland. Buyers can pick up their parcels from their chosen pick-up point or order home delivery for their purchases.

The business idea has been strengthened by the increase in online grocery shopping in 2020–2021 during the Covid pandemic as people invested in food delivery services.

> The strategic direction is the creation of something incrementally new for a familiar industry. In addition to food, the company sells clothing, home, sports, and health products, among others.
>
> A decisive competitive advantage is created in the minds of buyers when they can make substantial savings and reduce waste.
>
> **Fiksuruoka.fi**

Unikulma also sells sleep quality

At the heart of Unikulma's (Sleep Corner) competitive advantage is "personalised sleep". In practice, the company helps its customers to foster quality sleep with a wider business idea than selling a bed. A bed is, of course, important in fostering this mission. At Unikulma, a bed is built for the customer based on their individual needs. The company has developed the UnikLab® test, which measures the pressure produced by the body in bed. Using the pressure and shape maps displayed by the device and sleep analysis, experts tailor a personalised bed for each sleeper. The company uses physiotherapists and ergonomics experts to find optimal solutions for its customers.

Unikulma also offers interior design: ensuring a good night's sleep requires harmony between interior design and colours when falling asleep and waking up. Unikulma is Finland's leading bed manufacturer and retailer, as well as a sleep expert and researcher. The company started in the 1980s by selling items such as foam mattresses. Unikulma has been refining its business idea decade after decade. It is also a major player as a supplier of hotel, care, and hospital beds.

Strategic direction: re-shaping the company's activities or redefining its sector and focusing on the quality of sleep.

The competitive edge is a combination of decisive and strategic competitive advantages.

Unikulma.fi

B2B examples

HELTTI prevents

"We want to keep workers fit for work with preventive measures, not just treat those who are ill."

The promise of preventive action summarises the competitive advantage of Heltti as a provider of occupational health services.

Occupational health has traditionally focused on treating the sick. Heltti wants to take preventive care of its members, i.e., the employees of its client companies. It also highlights the need to look after the well-being of a growing pool of knowledge workers. In addition to maintaining and managing the customers' physical fitness, the company sees wellbeing in a broader sense as an important part of sustained fitness for work. Heltti emphasises the idea that a healthy and happy employee is the best option for all parties involved, including the employer.

Moreover, the traditional occupational health care system does not always meet the needs of today's knowledge worker, as mental health problems, exhaustion, and burnout are major causes of sick pay. Heltti defines its mission as being "an occupational health partner for knowledge workers".

Heltti also challenges the idea of the "traditional" pricing model. In a traditional performance-based pricing model, the interests of the client and the provider do not coincide: the more workers get sick, the better off the provider is financially.

Heltti has divided its services and pricing into three segments:

- sole entrepreneurs
- small businesses
- large businesses.

> The main strategic direction: Heltti creates something incrementally new for the industry. Heltti's competitors have also started to productise their services from a preventive perspective, but Heltti, as the first to move into this position, has a certain advantage.
>
> This is a decisive competitive advantage. The competitive edge and the business model and culture built on it are supportive of the competitive advantage. Developing knowledge capital into a competitive advantage can be seen in the case of Heltti. The competitive advantage is at the heart of the strategy and guides all activities. It will be difficult for a competitor to replicate the same way of working and culture. Heltti is also a good example of an excellent strategy with nothing to hide or be secretive about. It is transparent and clear.
>
> **Heltti.fi**

Noccela developed an alarm system that no one expected

Store alarm systems are something we are all familiar with: an alarm is attached to clothing, designed to alert when a shoplifter passes the alarm gates placed after the checkouts or around the exit.

Noccela ("Clever") wanted to create an alarm system that is based on location. When a theft attempt occurs, staff are informed by smartphone, which allows them to locate the perpetrator with an accuracy of 15 cm. So, Noccela did not make version 3.6 or 4.2 of the existing systems but instead created a completely new way of thinking that was quickly adopted.

On average, pilferage results in a loss of 2-4% of a store's profit. Noccela's promise is that there will be virtually no losses, so the losses can be transferred to the store's profit.

Another element of location-based technology is the use of the accumulated data for things like driving sales. Location can be used to improve customer service, and information from promotions at the store level can be used to plan the placement of goods, staff working hours, and so on. This development has also led to many other services where location can be utilized.

When a company introduces something unexpected into an existing market, the role of communications in taking the business idea to the market is especially significant. When people don't expect something, launching has its own challenges. This was also the case with Noccela.

> The strategic direction in this case is the creation of something radical new, which gives the company a strategic competitive advantage.

Noccela.com

Puucomp recreated itself

For decades, Oy Puucomp Ab manufactured plywood panels for the construction industry as a subcontractor. As demand collapsed due to a change in market structure, the company had to think about how to revive its business.

The company realised that in order to change, it needed to find a market-oriented perspective on planning its operations. It had to evolve from a production-oriented, invisible subcontractor to a customer-oriented one. Based on a thorough analysis of competitors, target groups, and the buying process, the company found a target group that it had not previously seen as potential: Finnish and international architectural firms that design a very specific type of building, demanding both visually and acoustically.

Communication and outreach were targeted at architects, following the wireframe model of strategic marketing. The key was

- finding value
- creating value
- communicating value.

The value creation process through these stages was a key cornerstone of market-oriented development. Target group segmentation was an essential part of finding a new direction. A more generic product-oriented message of "high-quality wood panels for demanding acoustic applications" would probably not have appealed to anyone.

Puucomp's traditional expertise turned into a strength when it started to look at things from a new perspective. With a marketing-driven approach, the company's sales increased by 35% in the first year, and the company also gained new customers in the Swedish market. Since then, the company has expanded its product range and reached new markets, and its stylish interior cladding panels can be seen in places like the interiors of Helsinki-Vantaa airport.

Puucomp is also an example of how a company can find new customers for its existing products by researching and analysing the market and its needs. In the case of Puucomp, this meant switching from an inside-out model to outside-in thinking. It sometimes makes sense to look at "traditional" competence in the light of the opportunities created by a changing environment.

> Strategic direction: the company reinvented itself. The company analysing its own competence, finding new markets, and adding value to products were the cornerstones of its success.
>
> A decisive competitive advantage: Strong product competence was refined into specialised competence. Product competence was also refined into service competence.
>
> **Puucomp.com**

Nordic Business Lab takes the customer into a more value-added B4B service business

Nordic Business Lab competes in the B2B market, and its customers are Finnish small and medium-sized technology companies with international growth potential. Typically, the companies manufacture hi-tech equipment such as sensors, production machines and production lines, or they provide technical services. The equipment and services go into the processes of large – mostly international – end customers, such as machinery component manufacturers, paper mills, car factories, and industrial plants.

In product sales, value creation is traditionally linked to the equipment or service sold. NBL's business idea is to build for its customers a new service business based on customer value.

NBL is encouraging its customers to think differently; it wants to help its customers see how much of their end customer's revenue goes through a machine rather than selling the machine itself. NBL builds a business for its clients based on tangible benefits to the end customer. The customer benefits are not only reflected in the sales message but also serve as a basis for things like pricing. When a benefit worth €100 is sold to the end customer, the price of the service is €20.

In practice, a customer's new service business includes not only a sales message and strategy but also new software to help the end customer streamline their processes or avoid failures. The idea is based on an insight from **Valtteri Tuominen**, the company's founder: when a company sells customer benefits, such as increased production rates or trouble-free production, sales are continuous and margins are multiplied.

The company starts by looking for a strategic position where the customer can add tangible value to the end customer in a way that "no one else in the world does". The company calls this superior customer benefit.

The methodology has been developed by the company. At best, it is a win-win-win model where everyone – the company, the customer and the customer's customer – wins. The customer's customer benefits, for example, through more efficient production. NBL has, therefore, abandoned the B2B model, where the seller earns based on the product sold. The company calls its methodology the B4B model, which sells ongoing benefits to the customer.

The strategic focus is on creating something incrementally new: the company helps the equipment supplier to create value through a continuous presence instead of just equipment sales. Often, the service takes the form of creating a digital service business. So, the company thinks differently from other equipment suppliers. NBL is still in its early days. Developing new thinking, taking it to the market, and opening it up to customers is a key part of business development.

A decisive competitive advantage: Valtteri Tuominen's market knowledge, education, and experience in working with international companies provide the necessary industry expertise to help him find and test new businesses at the customer interface. He is also the only person in Finland who has written a doctoral thesis on technology sales. Another competitive advantage is the ability of NBL's strong software development expertise to build from scratch the software required for a new service business. With this expertise, NBL is able to accompany the customer all the way from idea to pilot and from implementation to scaling up.

Businesslab.fi

Vincit invested in recruitment

Vincit, a Finnish company selling digital services, has grown into an international listed corporation but, when considering competitive advantage, it's worth looking back at the early days of the company.

Vincit started by trying to create a workplace "where you won't be annoyed coming to work on Monday". This bold statement comes from **Mikko Kuitunen**, the company's founder and CEO. It was based on the perception that there would be fierce competition for coders. Kuitunen saw that as an employer, he had to offer the best conditions to attract the best people. Recruiting top talent was key to the company's development and customer satisfaction. Even today, Vincit offers "more human digitalisation than usual".

> Strategic direction: to perceive the development of the industry. Vincit was competing for top talent and knew how to use a media-centred environment to ensure visibility and differentiation.
>
> A decisive competitive advantage: Vincit has consistently built a compelling employer image. It did so in the early days of the company and has continued to do so as it has grown into a listed company.
>
> **Vincit.fi**

Ellun Kanat repositioned itself

For many years, the position of the Ellun Kanat communications agency has been well known and respected. The name "Ellun Kanat" refers to a Finnish saying meaning carefree people. Founder **Kirsi Piha**'s long career in politics and experience gained through various media appearances have given the company a more prominent position among communications agencies than a traditional communications agency would receive. **Taru Tujunen**, the company's CEO, is also a former politician.

Ellun Kanat participates in social debate beyond the traditional role of a communications agency. Things like being aware of trends, conducting their own research and highlighting the need for change in companies, and networking with well-known people are essential to Ellun Kanat's business model. Its activities expand the perception of the role of a communications agency – and thereby also help to create new markets for its expertise.

Over time, Ellun Kanat has, therefore, made the need for change the focus of its activities and message. This positions it as a partner of management. The company's traditional competence, communication, is the competence needed to create and implement change. In addition to change management services, Ellun Kanat also offers its clients more traditional operational communications services.

> Strategic direction: the company creates something incrementally new in the industry by taking the lead in making changes.
>
> A decisive competitive advantage: Looking at the broader communications field, such as advertising, marketing, digital, communications, and media agencies, the market is often fragmented and over-saturated from a buyer's perspective. There seems to be more supply than demand. Ellun Kanat is positioning itself above traditional communications agencies. It also has a competitive advantage in the recognition of the company's well-known faces and social capital.
>
> Ellunkanat.fi

Superson puts together a dream team

There are many players in the field of marketing, advertising, digital, media and communications agencies. Competition is fierce, as there is far more supply than demand. The image of what is on offer is also often confused in the minds of buying customers due to the large number of services.

Digitalisation is rapidly changing the technological competence requirements of the industry in particular. Competence development is continuous. From the client's point of view, finding the right service provider is a challenge, especially if the buyer does not have in-depth knowledge of the market.

Superson's competitive advantage is to offer all the necessary marketing communication services on a one-stop-shop basis and in such a way that it can tailor a core team to the client's specific needs for each campaign or operation. Superson does not employ designers on the payroll. Rather, it has built a network from which it selects designers according to the client's needs.

The industry is so specialised that a good B2B designer is not necessarily the best choice to build a brand that works in the B2C market built on an image strategy. After all, the agencies offer, in a nutshell, the skills they have on their payroll. Companies also seek to partially optimise their customer relationships to ensure customer satisfaction. Superson's business idea offers a clear alternative to this.

Superson's project managers are in charge of projects and client relations. The creative team's talent is made up of experienced experts in different areas of design, such as art directors, digital specialists, analysts, copywriters, and graphic designers. Expert profiles (specialisations, industry experience, channel and medium experience, language skills, etc.) are predefined. Superson tailors each team to the client's needs. This ensures that the client has access to correct, up-to-date knowledge. Assignments are unpacked and implemented according to Superson's operating model.

> The strategic direction is market shaping. The competence already available on the market has been brought together in a single network. This gives the client access to a tailor-made team.
>
> The decisive competitive advantage is based on Superson's proprietary business idea and the business model derived from it.
>
> Superson.co

Wörks teams up with the customer

Wörks defines itself as a strategic marketing agency. Founded in 2011, the company took the agile methodologies that have since become a mantra for many companies – and put them into practice instead of just words.

Instead of a traditional model, where the client's team discusses solutions in its office, Wörks' founder Jaakko Veijola and partners created a model where the team went (and still goes) to the client's premises to work on the assignments they received – the principle being to grab a laptop and a briefcase and go.

The idea was to reduce the distance associated with the traditional way of working and to bring the team and the client closer together, in line with lean thinking. This meant that Wörks was more of a partner than a subcontractor. The flow of information is improved when silos are removed. The model also enables better client engagement for new proposals and collaborative work, as well as a smoother flow of information. Time is also used more efficiently through constant interaction.

Wörks' business model is based on self-direction. Since there are no planning managers in the Wörks model, those with customer responsibility must have sufficient experience as both planners and customer workers.

The company also realised from the start that taking a position in the market based on a new way of working requires good communication: even a great idea won't work if it doesn't find potential customers. **Jaakko Veijola**'s media artwork "Employment project Kalevi Pajatso" raised the profile of the company. The fictitious person Kalevi Pajatso sent a job application for all the job advertisements published in Helsingin Sanomat (Finland's leading newspaper) on a given day. With this and many other communication activities, Wörks achieved widespread publicity.

Now that Wörks has grown and prospered, it has continued to evolve: the company has received publicity for things like its four-day working week. The company believes in a need to balance the employees' personal and professional lives. Wörks declares that their staff is not allowed to work overtime. The underlying idea is that a mentally balanced employee will be able to enjoy work more and thus get more work done better and in less time. The company emphasises a "working culture based on humanity".

The strategic direction for Wörks is to create something incrementally new for the industry as customers' needs change. Wörks' approach could also be seen as observing changes in the industry and shaping its activities in line with new requirements. There is a lot of talk these days about agility, and that is what Wörks innovated. As the importance of marketing communication grows, marketers also have an increasing need for new ways of working together.

Wörks has a decisive competitive advantage. It challenged traditional business ideas in its industry through things like creating new ways of working with clients. It also knew how to use distinctive communication to make its case from the start.

Wörks.fi

Leadoo Marketing Technologies finds out online visitors' needs and contact details

Leadoo Marketing Technologies is a martech company founded in 2018 that has quickly established a clear and respected position in the market. Leadoo MT's idea is to convert visitors to its clients' websites into tangible leads or online sales by engaging visitors through chatbots and other toolkits.

The idea behind Leadoo MT is to create more conversions by adding activating elements on the client's website when a potential customer visits the company's website. For example, Leadoo uses chatbots to make a needs assessment of the website visitor's situation. It tries to create a dialogue – and eventually "kindly" asks for the visitor's contact details. In this way, Leadoo has created a lead for the client, identifying the customer's needs and contact details.

Leadoo MT is basically a marketing automation platform, but its innovation is the software that, through dialogue, collects "hot" processed lead data for further use by the client. The software used in the platform is the result of in-house development.

The customer gets full access to the Leadoo platform. They can then build as many bots as they feel they need. This is one of Leadoo's competitive advantages.

For a start-up, Leadoo has got off to a flying start: it has operations in Finland and other European countries.

> Strategic alignment can be seen as both creating something incrementally new and shaping the company's activities in the face of industry change. There are several marketing automation platforms on the market. Leadoo brought to the table its own idea that allows sales to get hot leads through "shortcuts". There are many players in the martech segment, and new ones are constantly emerging. Leadoo used a bypass lane to offer a clear alternative to existing players.
>
> Leadoo's competitive edge is a decisive competitive advantage. Leadoo offers its clients a different, Finnish platform with a clearly communicable promise.
>
> **Leadoo.com**

Other company examples

Under this heading are the companies that operate in both the B2B and B2C segments.

Bellylabs developed a home pregnancy test for dogs

An innovation developed by Bellylabs allows a dog's pregnancy to be determined at home.

Usually, pregnancy is determined by an ultrasound examination performed by a veterinarian. In visual inspection, the traditional way of assessing the possible pregnancy of a dog is to observe the dog's appearance, behaviour, and appetite.

The Bellylabs test is similar to a coronavirus self-test or a human pregnancy test. A blood sample is taken from the dog's gum and immersed in a sample vial and then in a test cartridge. The result is ready in 15 minutes and has an accuracy level of 96%.

Compared to ultrasound, the Bellylabs method has the advantage of being cheaper, as well as being easy, stress-free and fast. The dog is only needed for a minute to do the test.

> Bellylabs' strategic direction is to create something incrementally new. Its methodology has provided a cheaper and easier-to-perform alternative to the commonly used ultrasound examination. The competitive edge is either a strategic or decisive competitive advantage. The company has (at the time of writing) applied for a patent on certain parts of its test method.
>
> **Belly-labs.com**

NAMS tomatoes proved it
– bulk can make for a quality product

Tomatoes are enjoyed all year round, whatever the season. Tomatoes consumed in the Nordic countries during the dark season are mainly imported.

In winter, people miss the taste and flavour of domestically grown vegetables, which are usually only available in summer. NAMS ("YUM") tomatoes meets this challenge by producing tomatoes all year round in its own greenhouse using state-of-the-art technology.

From the perspective of differentiation, the most important thing about NAMS Tomatoes is their taste. Varieties are chosen for their flavour: maximizing production volumes is not the most important factor. The company does not use spray pesticides because they damage the flavour of the tomato skin. The tomatoes are hand-picked to minimize bruises and are only picked when they are ripe and delicious. To optimise the taste experience, the products are quickly delivered to the tomato shelves of local grocery stores for sale. Due to the processing chain, the price per kilo of NAMS Tomatoes is, of course, higher than that of regular tomatoes.

> The strategic direction is to create something incrementally new. Of course, this requires the segmentation of target groups, both in stores and among consumers. Transparency and responsibility are part of the brand.
>
> A decisive competitive advantage is the quality-branding of domestic tomatoes. The company will continue to develop its activities on the basis of the experience gained. This way, it seeks to further develop its competitive advantage and business idea.
>
> Nams.fi

Woodio uses recyclable wood material and combines it with Nordic design

Woodio develops and manufactures fully water-resistant wood composite products, such as integrated washbasins for kitchens and bathtubs and sinks for private and public use. All products are based on Nordic design.

The term 'wood composite' means that the products are made from wood chips using technology developed by Woodio. The company obtains wood chips from Metsä Group's production side streams. Side stream materials are left over from the production process of a main product. Woodio manufactures long-lasting value-added products from surplus materials – and thus supports recycling with its business idea. Responsibility permeates the entire life cycle of the products, from the recovery of materials to the product, use, and disposal.

> The strategic direction is to create something incrementally new. Recognisable design is an essential part of the brand.
>
> A decisive competitive advantage: When buying a Woodio product, the buyer buys both the idea of wood composite products and Nordic design.
>
> **Woodio.fi**

Solar Foods produces protein from carbon dioxide and electricity

Solar Foods Oy produces a new type of nutrient-rich protein using only air and electricity. Its competitive advantage is based on research projects conducted by the Technical Research Centre of Finland VTT Oy and Lappeenranta University of Technology (LUT), which verified the viability of the high-protein food production concept.

The Solar Foods concept redefines the basis of food production, which is not dependent on agriculture, weather, or climate. In addition, the price of the protein product is competitive compared to alternatives like soy protein.

The company is in its early stages, but investors and owners believe it can produce protein in a cost-competitive, scalable way. The company's aim is to develop a high-quality protein product with an environmental impact 10 to 100 times lower than the meat or meat substitutes currently on the market.

> The strategic direction is to create something radical new that no one expects or lacks.
>
> A radical competitive advantage: The idea of protein made with air and electricity is, of course, theoretically "stealable". But, as is so often the case in similar cases, the pioneering operator gains an advantage. With this idea, media attention is also relatively easy to achieve.
>
> **Solarfoods.com**

COMPETITIVE ADVANTAGE PUT INTO PRACTICE

> **Company culture is the air that employees and customers breathe.**

Kari Korkiakoski, Customer Experience Specialist

We have arrived at the Blue Ocean. The stormiest and most challenging phase is behind us. There are no competitors in sight, but there is still work to be done.

The next step is to put this competitive advantage into practice. First, we should consider how competitive advantage can be placed at the heart of our strategy. What is the role of competitive advantage in strategy? I will also define our brand – and integrate the company into one great entity through the brand. And how do we create a new culture now that a competitive edge has been found? The intention is also to knock down silos (which are only needed for certain in nuclear power plants).

How do we communicate the good news of a unique innovation within the organisation and to the market? I will introduce practical tips on how to turn a product-oriented, generic promise into an elevator pitch and an appealing, customer-oriented promise.

But as always: the terrain is different from the map. Competitive advantage must be put into practice. The idea is that the company creates the best version of itself.

Competitive advantage is at the heart of strategy

> Competitive advantage is at the heart of the success of a company operating in a free market.

Michael E. Porter

Small business elevator pitch

For a small business, the company's competitive advantage is its elevator pitch, the Midas touch that sets the company apart from the rest and appeals to the target audience. It allows the company to take its future into its own hands.

For a smaller company, an elevator pitch is often sufficient for internal and external use. It's easier to keep a smaller work community together and up-to-date when the "team" is in the same room. Business plans and strategies, and how they work in everyday life, are in the entrepreneur's head – and, therefore, easier to communicate. The concept of a business idea in the recesses of an entrepreneur's mind can be more coherent and powerful than a hundred-page report with spreadsheets and graphs from a listed company. In a small company, a common script is easier to keep available on a daily basis.

> Securing a competitive advantage is a critical success factor for any successful business.

Marina Vahtola, board professional and successful business leader

I understand very well what we stand for.

I feel that I'm not talking past the customer.

It's nice when the customer wants to ask clarifying questions.

Competitive advantage put into practice

Growth requires a strategy

As companies grow to double-digit headcounts, there is an increasingly urgent need for a strategy – or whatever you want to call it – to manage the business. This is about the short- and long-term decisions taken at the top to ensure the intellectual, social, and economic well-being of the company.

As I mentioned with disappointment earlier, strategy as a term has become stale. It's not the strategy's fault; it's the fault of strategy designers. The strategies that are written as strategies are tired and empty – more like "barrels of empty hopes". Strategies such as "We want to grow by 15% in the next few years" do not contain the hard core of titanium that can drive the growth target. Empty barrels are hardly a driver for development and leadership. You can't take water out of an empty bucket.

Heart and brain

This book is framed in such a way that competitive advantage is a key part of the strategy of a growing and developing company. It is the heart and brain of the company. For growing small businesses and SMEs, a competitive advantage is the key to policy formulation. It allows the company to compete in a free market and believe that success will come in both the short and long term. It is a key guidance and management toolkit. Competitive advantage, as well as the strategy and business model derived from it, are the factors that allow a company to interact with markets and stakeholders. For a larger company, competitive advantage lies in its core offering of products and services. It is used by management, HR, communications, sales, customer service, marketing, and product development alike.

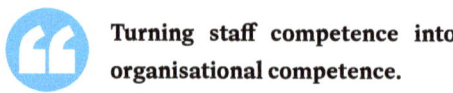

Turning staff competence into organisational competence.

COMPETITIVE ADVANTAGE AS A DRIVER FOR ORGANISATIONAL DEVELOPMENT

There is a lot of talk about change. Creating change requires leadership. But what does leadership require? In this chapter, our starting point is the idea that a company's staff and its competence are the drivers of change, guided by a competitive advantage or strategy. By combining the competence and strategy of the people, we give ourselves a chance to solemnly declare:

A strategy is only a strategy when it influences the thoughts and actions of everyone in the company – and therefore also its customers and stakeholders.

You can't go for an innovative outcome if the starting idea is not radical.

Are we doing the right things?

Competitive advantage and the strategy built on it are an untapped asset for companies: a card that has not yet been turned. This is due to the industrial model and the thinking that has come out of it, which has influenced the way things have been shaped. Competitive advantage wants to challenge and ask questions:

 When individuals have a lot of competence, companies do things right. But we can ask whether the right things are being done.

Companies have intellectual, skill-based, tactical, technical, and operational competence. Competence is updated as necessary. We are increasingly competent in our own individual skills. So, we know how to "do things right".

"Doing the right things" is the angle that competitive advantage is putting on the table in this debate. When a company finds a common plot, a common thread, a script, the management of human capital will also find its direction.

For example, Heltti, a provider of occupational health services, has a business idea and strategy based on competitive advantage, which is: "We want to keep workers fit for work through preventive measures, not just treat those who are ill."

So, Heltti has a clear policy on what it competes in, what its competitive field is, and who its target groups are. It has defined its areas of competence, as per the anatomy of a good strategy. Heltti's business concept is also a clear and transparent basis for the development of individuals in the organisation, the orientation of teams in terms of competence, the development of the company's offering, and recruitment.

Heltti raises the question of what a company should be able to do as a whole (not just at the individual and functional level). The business idea created from a competitive advantage provides a context for the development of individuals, teams, and the whole. Competitive advantage is the direction of change that drives the development of human capital collectively. This also puts the company's education budget in a new perspective.

Develop individuals, teams, and culture as a whole within the framework of competitive advantage (Figure 3).

Figure 3. Developing an organisation based on competitive advantage.

As the importance of teamwork grows, silos will have to come down. The knowledge work's idea of working together and creating value together is better realised. Doing so will create a new culture. The specifics always depend on the individual, functions, team, and company. The human capital and resources in a company are the basis for its development.

In this way, individuals, functions, and "doing things right" are also refined into "doing the right things" because the business idea drives development and change. A rear-wheel drive becomes a four-wheel drive, an individual sport becomes a team sport.

The holistic, collective approach could be described by an analogy from theatre, film, or literature: when a company has a common plot, a common thread, it also has the potential to create a clear script in which everyone plays their part for the good of the whole. Competence development is development towards a particular competence.

The idea is, therefore, to develop a culture based on the value proposition (business idea) of the individual, the function, the team, and the partners.

 Competence has little value if it is not managed. Competence is more valuable (and profitable) when managed holistically.

In Heltti's case, one can clearly see that this strategic concept has been implemented. Increasingly, companies need to create value (including value for investments) through people's competence. Developing common competence requires finding a common script. If it cannot be found, there are plenty of whistlers in the organisation who can certainly whistle well. The only thing missing is a common tune.

Developing common competence requires finding a common script.

The overall development of a company is different from the development of individuals within a company. Let's use a football analogy: The coaches of a football team have decided on a certain way of playing (a business idea). Defensive players (individuals) learn how to implement this way of playing as a team. The defensive line (function) plays together as the way of playing requires. Midfielders playing above the defenders learn the same individual and functional play for each area of the game. These, in turn, link their skills to the offensive players. In this way, all individuals and groups are trained to implement a common way of playing (a business idea).

Anyone who has watched a peewee team play has noticed that every player runs after the ball in a disorganised and scrambling fashion. Everyone wants to touch the ball. It certainly looks fun and passionate. As the peewees grow and their skills develop, their training to become team players begins. Time will come later for them to learn to play as individuals and as a team.

A new business should have passion (without it, it is difficult to be successful). At the root of passion lies attitude. When passion is awakened, so is attitude. To succeed, you should have the passion to develop something of your own. With twenty passionate entrepreneurs with a burning desire to run a café and space for only five new businesses on the market, most end up with nothing. Finding "your thing" is central and important.

You don't have to be the best because there is no such thing as "the best" in absolute terms. It is better to have a moderate plan today than a perfect plan the day after tomorrow.

A BRAND IS A JOINT CREATION BY THE CUSTOMER AND THE COMPANY

The book has now reached the stage where we already know our competitive advantage. So far, we have gone through and learned something that has the ingredients of a clearly thought-out elevator pitch and the essence of a strategy.

Following the wireframe model, we move on to the value creation phase, where even the abstract idea of competitive advantage is further refined into a business idea and business model. If, for example, the competitive advantage of a café is large cinnamon rolls, this insight needs to be implemented and translated into daily operations. How are the cinnamon rolls made? What should the baking rhythm be? Where do you get the ingredients to make them? What is the secret of their taste? How do you present them and make them attractive? Are they intended for one person, or are you selling the idea of the customer bringing a friend? What do you want to offer with them? How is the customer experience of enjoying baked goods in a café? And how does the promise hold up when the cinnamon roll is enjoyed at home or at work?

When developing a business model, there are many questions. Good answers come when you take action. The competitive advantage is the foundation and the guide.

However, we will not discuss the business model here any further. Instead, we will continue towards communications following the path set out by the wireframe model. Even the best idea can't exist if you are not able to communicate it both internally and to the market – to the target groups and stakeholders.

Defining the brand

Between the business idea and the customers, the biggest common denominator is the brand. Defining your brand is the first step in planning your communication. It is based on the found value / target group on which the competitive advantage is based (i.e., not on one's personal preferences).

The need to define the brand applies to both start-ups and existing businesses. In the case of an existing business, once a competitive advantage has been found, it needs to be repositioned and rebranded.

© Vierula Consulting 2024
M. Vierula, *Find Your Market-Oriented Competitive Advantage*,
https://doi.org/10.1007/978-3-031-71663-8_10

The primary function of a brand is to deliver value to its customers. So, in this context, it's not just a visual look or a nice-sounding slogan. The brand is the identity of the company, the key value driver that the staff works for every day. A brand is what the market values and what brings value to customers. A brand is a joint creation by the customer and the company.

Various toolkits will help you define your brand. Their use ensures that the definition of the brand and the values it generates are understood in the same way throughout the organisation. When the significance of the brand and its purpose are internalised consistently throughout the organisation, from the customer interface to management, the outward communication at all levels will also be more consistent and disciplined in building the brand.

One of the tasks of a brand is to summarize the essential in a way that appeals to the target group. Defining the brand and designing its visuality, functionality, and content will also help customers to distinguish and recognise the brand from the noise and communications around them. Definition ensures consistency. The brand contains the values of the company. It guides the management, service design, sales, development, and customer experience. A well-defined brand value is also the basis for a yearly plan for communications and all other actions.

From an internal perspective, a brand is a management toolkit that guides messages, actions, style, content, channels, and product development. It is a common denominator among everyone in the organisation. From this perspective, we are talking about a holistic brand concept.

Not everyone can be a brand

You can't just decide to be a brand. Brands grow and develop along a certain path. You've certainly sometimes set your gaze on the starry sky in the darkness of the night. In a cloudless sky, you may see stars as far as the eye can see, hundreds and hundreds of them. They all look the same. Except for Sirius and a few other stars that look bigger and brighter than others. A similar phenomenon of differentiation also applies to brands.

The vast majority of so-called brands are, in fact, products, labels, and branded products. They are a large set of products and services that do not differ much from the point of view of their target groups. Many of them are certainly good and of high quality, but they are still just labels and branded products. Figure 4 illustrates the path from product to brand.

You become a brand by following a certain path:

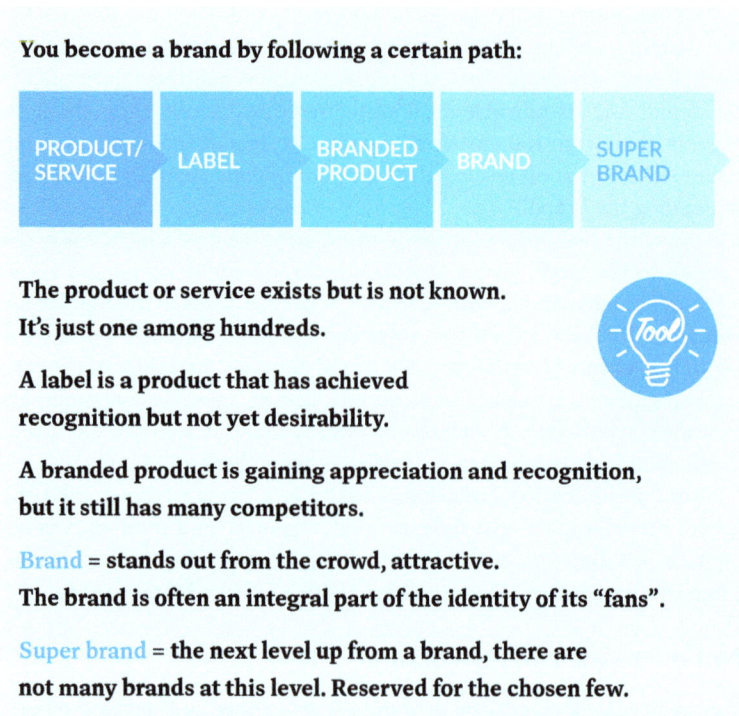

The product or service exists but is not known. It's just one among hundreds.

A label is a product that has achieved recognition but not yet desirability.

A branded product is gaining appreciation and recognition, but it still has many competitors.

Brand = **stands out from the crowd, attractive.
The brand is often an integral part of the identity of its "fans".**

Super brand = **the next level up from a brand, there are not many brands at this level. Reserved for the chosen few.**

Figure 4. Developing and growing into a brand.

Re-branding an existing business

A competitive advantage can also be found for an existing company, as the company cases show. Once found, the next step is to define the brand and its functional, contentual, and visual design. This is a necessary step if a company wants to take a new position in the market. Fine-tuning an old, tried-and-tested look or a superficial tweak will not send out a strong enough message about the new promise. The same applies to the mission statement and slogan. Many people already have an impression of an existing company, so it is important to make it part of the objective to break the old perception in order to make room for a new and better one. A new position must be taken over. Without branding and communication, it won't be possible.

Avoid these adjectives

Avoid the traditional brand definitions of "agile" or "approachable" or "transparent" or "sustainable" or "nice guy" or "this and that fun". They are easy to fall back on. They are good values in practical or operational terms, but they do not help to win a place in the mind and heart of the customer. They lack identity, distinctiveness, and personality. Without real depth, they remain a light form of branding. Light branding is intellectual self-deception. It's a bit like going to the gym to just sit on the machines or do nothing but biceps and imagining that your fitness will improve that way. Light branding leaves the company at the label level, which often means anonymity.

What brand isn't or doesn't want to be approachable and agile? Those adjectives are often only hygiene factors, the basic conditions that allow you to participate in the competition. Sustainability, transparency, and approachability must be in place to even participate credibly in the game. They are competitiveness factors. There will be no decisive or differentiating breakaway with, say, sustainability, unless we are talking about Plan, the Red Cross, the Baltic Sea Action Group, the WWF or similar non-profit organisations. Solar Foods (p. 104), a radical innovator, is an example of a future commercial brand for which sustainability is a compelling core value.

More and more brands want to be sustainable, to find meaning. That's good. However, this does not yet guarantee a competitive advantage. Meaningfulness is often a hygiene factor. The optimal level of ambition is to achieve an equation that implements the sustainability + competitiveness advantage model. This combines meaning and a competitive edge. Solar Foods is implementing the sustainability + competitiveness advantage equation in an exemplary manner. The same sustainability + competitiveness advantage formula is also implemented by companies such as restaurant Nolla, FabPatch, ReLove, Rekki, and Lovia. Mastering this equation contains the conditions for an optimally successful business.

The fast lane to branding opens up with a competitive advantage

Growing from a branded product to a brand is the most demanding part of this growth path. To become a brand, you have to look beyond the whole range of branded products and brands that are already there. There is no shortcut to growing to a brand.

The opportunity to use the fast lane comes from finding a competitive advantage. If you create something new and superior, you have the potential to become a brand faster. With a competitive advantage, the route is more or less the same, but the pace is faster. Armed with a competitive advantage – and good communication – a company takes off majestically like an eagle from a treetop.

 So, when defining a brand, it's a good idea to turn on the lane departure warning system: that way, the customer perspective stays in focus.

A good wine deserves a good wine glass. The glass helps to bring out the aromas and flavours. As in all professional work, proper toolkits are essential when defining a brand.

Defining functional brand values, core values, and a compelling value based on a unique position are prerequisites for redeeming a competitive advantage in practice. Once a brand has been defined using a three-dimensional toolkit, the foundation for designing compelling communications has been laid.

"Of cruose we sevre thees cutsomres thogetre"

A brand that is as refined as possible integrates the whole organisation and serves as a management toolkit. In this way, the brand is its own autonomous entity, representing the voice of the customer within the organisation.

Once the brand has been defined, it's time to move on to planning your communications.

The brand integrates the whole, internally and externally.

Integrate the whole organisation with a brand

Competitive advantage and the brand derived from it are like an umbrella under which the organisation can be integrated to operate holistically. The competitive advantage is the helm and coordinates for the navigation bridge. Integration, the promotion of team play, takes place at the level of thinking, defined values, and culture. A competitive advantage, or in a growing company, a strategy based on competitive advantage, is the concrete foundation for this. Developing collective competence and creating new ways of thinking and working creates a common, clear identity. By defining the brand and integrating its activities, the company strives to be internally and externally made of the same hardwood.

Power and turf battles, different ways of leading, and different goals should all be subservient to a common script. This will make the competence in the company more effective and create a clearer direction and, as a result, clearer management.

When the significance of a competitive advantage and the brand derived from it and its purpose are internalised consistently throughout the organisation, from the customer interface to the management, the outward communication at all levels will also be more consistent and disciplined in building the brand. Competitive advantage also drives the customer experience at all levels.

Integration is not just about working together but also about learning together.

Make the brand a band

A brand is an overarching idea that unites all the company's activities and the philosophy that guides all its actions. A holistic approach and its successful management require orchestration. A common composition and arrangement and a shared understanding of the responsibilities and roles of individuals and functions help to create a brand that works like a top band.

A brand built to be competitive also integrates the company internally; only an internally strong company can be externally strong and consistent.

There is a lot of talk these days about self-direction. To achieve optimal self-direction, individuals need to understand the underlying idea of what the organisation is about – and their role in it. When the brand is well-defined (with rational and emotional values), it also helps the staff to better internalize the business idea, thus avoiding an old-fashioned top-down implementation. A good goal is to "rationalize" the brand and help everyone involved to understand the brand at all levels, rather than the traditional top-down implementation. When an individual understands the purpose of doing something, and when there are also emotional factors involved, commitment to work increases and motivation is at a more significant level – and thus, productivity at work increases.

A strategy defines the company's goals. Equally, the strategy defines the means and approaches that will be used to achieve the goals. The implementation phase of the strategy involves taking the strategy to all levels of the organisation. To do this successfully, the strategy needs to be refined for use in communication. The more personal the communication, the better the chances of success. The more deeply emotional elements are involved, the more the individual will contribute to the organisation.

Viable, coherent strategic communication is born from a strategy based on a competitive advantage.

It is difficult to organize a crowd scene by yourself. Promoting integration is, therefore, not only about working together but also about learning together. It is a step towards an organisation that focuses on developing collective competence (rather than developing individuals and functions). A hierarchical, fragmented organisation is not conducive to the joint development of multi-talents. This is why breaking down silos is a key development activity.

Figure 5. Organization wrapped around customers

Barriers to change

Naturally, the transition to a new, integrated approach faces obstacles. It may arouse internal resistance. It is not easy to break down silos because companies are also living in bubbles. The traditional way of developing separate strategies for each function and channel, decentralised organisational structure, and the budgeting that underpins them are challenging and formidable wrestling partners. Once prejudices, internal status competitions, and many other emotional problems have been overcome and bubbles have been burst, the conditions have been created for the development of the organisation's team play.

COMMUNICATION

The brand, a key element of communication, is now defined. The organisation is working and developing together.

Even the best idea can't exist if you are not able to communicate it both internally and to the market. If there are a hundred products or services on the market (and there are at least that many), they cannot all be brands. The vast majority of these are products, labels, or branded products. The supply is plentiful. It exceeds demand. The noise level in the market is reminiscent of the souks of Marrakesh storytellers. There is a lot of noise and many sales pitches, each one more colourful than the next. Everything is very tempting. Without compelling communication, even a company with a good competitive advantage will remain a nice academic exercise. The best friend of compelling communication is creativity.

With the vigour provided by a competitive advantage, a company – whether a start-up or an existing business – is ready to enter the market. With a brand built on this competitive advantage, communication can be more coherently planned and executed. There is a clear direction through the definition of a competitive advantage and branding. This also makes it easier to define the goals of communication. A competitive advantage provides a fast lane to brand growth. A business idea enriched with a competitive advantage already creates a decisive, differentiating, and recognisable framework from the customer's perspective. There is always demand for a superior innovation that solves the customer's problems.

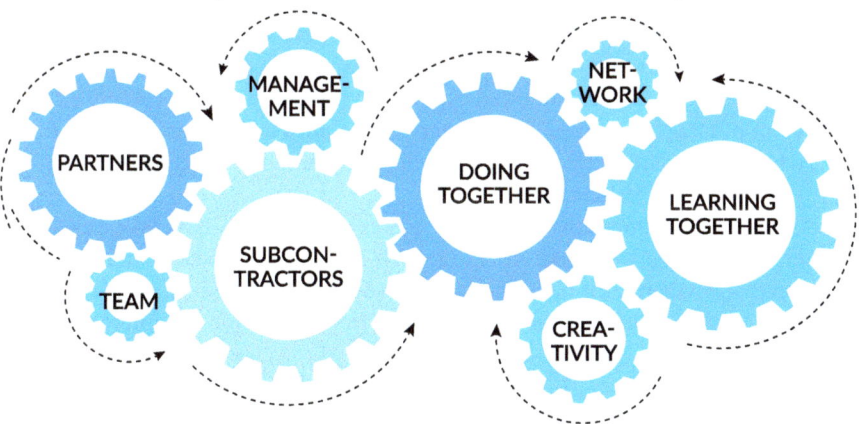

Figure 6. The cogwheels of individuals, teams, networks, and stakeholders are turned with communication.

© Vierula Consulting 2024
M. Vierula, *Find Your Market-Oriented Competitive Advantage*,
https://doi.org/10.1007/978-3-031-71663-8_11

When a company uses a competitive advantage to create a superior offering, it is "easier" to design and produce a communication concept and message, as there is little risk of the results of the communication falling into the hands of a competitor. In addition, brand recognition can be ensured. Of course, the brand competes for attention amidst all the noise, but when the brand idea is original, it offers a more impressive platform for ensuring recognition in terms of both content and visual appeal.

Communication is an essential skill throughout the organisation – and from the organisation outwards. Communication extends its tentacles in many directions. I am not going to lecture on communication from the perspective of communicating a competitive advantage. Instead, I will present a few concrete examples of a good elevator pitch. The concept behind this example-based presentation is that through creative thinking and creative writing, we are going to translate a few product-oriented elevator pitches into market-oriented ones.

How to write an elevator pitch

Writing an elevator pitch is a challenge. The promise should be compressed to an elevator length, which probably means a ten-floor elevator ride and a 30-second sales pitch. You can't fit many sentences into that. This is a particular challenge if the company does not have what might be called "their thing".

In the absence of a competitive advantage, many companies' elevator pitches are also made to fit the spirit of the times. "Good vibes! Lean and laid back! We're the best!" declare the sales pitches of many companies. As part of the product-oriented tradition, it is traditional to write the elevator pitch in "we" form. The problem often comes with the essential part: what is the solution by the company that is appealing – let alone superior – in the eyes of the customer?

Here, too, competitive advantage comes to the rescue. Let's take a closer look at what a product-oriented and a market-oriented elevator pitch looks like when built on a competitive advantage for the same offering. Here are a few before-and-after solutions from companies in different industries.

A company that sells hydraulic lifting equipment

Product-oriented elevator pitch:

We have a wide range of lifting equipment to meet your company's different needs.

Competitive advantage-driven elevator pitch:

We provide our customers with superior lifting solutions by integrating up-to-date weather data as a service into our products. This is also how we help our customers' customers in their business activities.

A company that develops and markets IT maintenance services

Product-oriented elevator pitch:

Smart IT solutions with professionalism. Skilled professionals.

Competitive advantage-driven elevator pitch:

The service process we have developed ensures the continuity of our customers' production process by detecting and reacting before interruptions occur.

A company that develops solutions to reduce shop wastage

Product-oriented elevator pitch:

We have created a completely new solution to reduce shop wastage.

Competitive advantage-driven elevator pitch:

With our localisation technology, we can reduce your store's wastage by 2–4%, which the store can pass on directly to the bottom line.

So, the customer perspective is key. The foundation is an understanding of the customer's concerns. Or it could be an idea of what the customer could do better. When a company talks about a customer's business challenges and how to solve them in a new way, the customer is also interested in learning more about the topic. (The same formula that works at the bar when you want to impress someone. Talk about them, not yourself. It is said to arouse more interest in the listener.)

A good elevator pitch requires good wording. If creating the idea behind the slogan – the competitive advantage – is challenging, so is writing the slogan. The slogan has its own requirements, of which an economical use of words and the ability to dramatize are the most challenging.

Toolkit

The essential anatomy of a slogan is that it contains

- a promise based on competitive advantage
- a crystallized meaning for the target group
- a dramatization of the product or service in a distinctive way.

It is also essential that

- you can build long-term content on the slogan
- the content is linked to the slogan
- the slogan works both internally and externally.

Rhetorically, slogans should be written with ambition. If a company has found its competitive advantage, it must also be able to express it in a way that stands out (specifically in the minds of the chosen target group), makes an impression, and sticks in mind. Creativity and the associated ambition to strive for excellence are key to writing an elevator pitch and a slogan. On the other hand, if you've managed to find a competitive advantage, the slogan itself is only half-finished without dramatization. Creative writing is a key skill here.

Here's an excellent example of a good slogan and a crystallization of the meaning of organisation:

We are Ladies and Gentlemen serving Ladies and Gentlemen

In its philosophy, the Ritz-Carlton Hotel takes a strong stance on not only its customer promise but also the kind of employee it wants to have in its ranks. The slogan also expresses the hotel's position in a magnificent way. The promise works internally and externally.

The definition of good communication: it brings value to both the sender and the recipient of the message.

The transmission of information is not the desired outcome of communication. In the context of a business, the essential goal is to have an impact (derived from strategy) at the level of information, action, or emotion. A good communicator knows how to set these goals for themselves depending on the situation.

Toolkit

The definition of good communication: good communication brings value to both the sender and the receiver.

In order to achieve this noble two-way objective, communication must:

- be relevant to the target group from the recipient's point of view
- promote the idea of a better way or competitive advantage
- be appealing in terms of both content and style
- be served through the right channel, in the right format.

For the sender, these criteria are met when the communication:

- is consistent, based on a competitive advantage or strategy
- is brand-building
- highlights issues that are relevant and topical
- also appeals to the company's own people.

> **As the importance of brands grows, so does the importance of communication. As the importance of communication grows, so does the importance of brand management.**

> **As the importance of brand management grows, so does the importance of managing target groups, stakeholders, messages, channels, and encounters.**

SUMMARY

- Use your competitive advantage to develop the collective competence of the whole organisation; a competitive advantage is a driver for developing collective competence.

- A brand plays many roles. It is the biggest common denominator between the company, its stakeholders, and its customers. The role of a brand is to bring value to both the company and its fans. The value of a brand is determined by the target group.

- Integrate all functions internally around customers and stakeholders.

- Through a brand, the organisation becomes a tightly knit band.

- Understand the need to develop team play and break down prejudices and misconceptions that hinder team play.

- Not all products, services and companies can be brands. The competitive advantage gives the opportunity to develop faster as a brand.

- Communication based on competitive advantage is one of the company's success factors. With the help of competitive advantage, the company also aligns the implementation of communication, internally and externally.

PART III: FOOD FOR THOUGHT

In this section, we will go through the essential themes that will help you find your competitive advantage and put it into practice. The idea is still to expand our thinking and use a machete to make room for new ideas. Creative thinking and creative work are among the most important factors in creating something new.

We will also look at how competitive advantage fits in with modern isms and toolkits such as digitalisation, customer experience, growth hacking, story-driven branding, service design, modern sales, lean, and marketing automation.

All known strategy toolkits are grouped together at the end of Part III. The toolkits that have been categorised under the headings "Toolkits for creating something new" and "Toolkits for developing resources" (in the spirit of the book) are presented in more detail. The strong position of traditional product-oriented thinking is underlined by the fact that most known toolkits do not deal with the creation of new things.

INNOVATION REQUIRES CREATIVITY

In this chapter, I discuss the essential competence needed to find a competitive advantage. In order to succeed, businesses need constant creativity: creative thinking, creative processes, and creative breakthroughs.

 **Innovation can only happen if the starting point is radical.**

Creative work is important

Marketing agencies, theatres, science, galleries, publishing houses, architecture firms, restaurants, design agencies, and many other businesses and industries thrive on creative work. Creativity and the results of creative work play a key role in creating value for all of us every day. Creative thinking and business activities in the creative industries also have a huge impact on the economy. Creativity creates growth, productivity, and innovation.

From a marketing perspective, creativity in business is often associated with advertising and marketing communications, planning, and execution. Standing out from the crowd has required creative solutions. That's good. Creative skills and creative solutions will continue to play an important role in the creation and development of brands.

We need business creativity

Creativity is the competence used to create innovations. Discovering and creating something new requires creativity, just as Kotler's definition of strategic marketing on page xx says: "The art and science…"

In order to identify roles and meanings, let's make a distinction between different definitions of creativity. In the search for a competitive advantage, the concept of creativity is given a much-needed update, for example with the compound word business creativity. A more descriptive term is strategic creativity. This refers to the creativity that generates new competitive advantages, business ideas, and innovations. Business creativity is located at the beginning of the wireframe model based on Kotler's definition of strategic marketing (see page xx), at its left-hand edge. It belongs to the stage where value is sought and something new and superior is created, and to the stage in the value chain before communication.

© Vierula Consulting 2024
M. Vierula, *Find Your Market-Oriented Competitive Advantage*,
https://doi.org/10.1007/978-3-031-71663-8_12

Business creativity, or strategic creativity, focuses on finding and creating a competitive advantage, on the basis of which communication (in a broad sense) is also designed: whether it is a new restaurant concept, developing a service and culture within a company into a competitive advantage, or refining a start-up's technological innovation into a market-oriented direction.

Creative marketing communication, on the other hand, is about bringing a competitive advantage or business idea to the market in a clear and expressive way in the eyes and minds of the target groups. When a business idea has its own creative storyline, consistent communication planning and production are also on a stronger footing. The risk of producing bland and boring communications is reduced.

Wide-ranging creative competence

Creativity includes creative work, creative thinking, and the final creative product or service. We must realise that creativity is needed at various points along the way when looking for a creative breakthrough. Problem-solving, critical thinking, and adaptability to change are typical prerequisites of creative thinking and action.

Creativity is a conceptually abstract and complex phenomenon. The concepts of creativity and "being creative" are ambiguous and difficult to decipher. Related concepts include intelligence, imagination, invention, problem-solving, and innovation. Creativity covers everything from an individual's personal everyday creativity to finding and developing a radical creative solution.

Creativity stinks of sweat

To find a competitive edge, you need a strong spirit and the courage to think outside the box. The hardest and perhaps most confusing part is challenging your own thinking and views. Product-oriented thinking is firmly embedded in us. Innovation can only happen if the starting point is radical. Without the courage to challenge your own ideas, it is difficult to get started in creating something new.

Secondly, you need the desire to create something new and the attitude to discover something new. Thirdly, creativity is required because it is always creativity that is needed to create something new. No matter how hard and uncompromising one's spirit and desire, they are not enough to achieve a good result. Without creative solutions, there can be no breakthroughs in a "ready-made world, in a crowded market where everything is already available". Without creativity, there will be nothing superior, new, and interesting.

By definition, an innovation is a solution that offers something completely new or partly new. The underlying idea is that if a competitive advantage does not bring something new to the market, either slightly better (incrementally new) or completely unprecedented (radical new), one cannot talk about an innovative, creative solution – which is always a prerequisite for a competitive advantage.

Creativity is raw, goal-oriented work. Often it stinks of sweat.

A creative solution must be unique. According to Nando Malmelin and Petro Poutanen, who have written on organisational creativity, it must contain a unique idea that will "change and improve the industry" in some way. In a business framework, the creative idea or product must contain an essential new element (incremental) or be superior (radical), especially for customers and stakeholders. This can take the form of improving existing products or developing new products. It can be an adaptation to the status quo, producing something new by doing something familiar but bringing something new to it. Or it can be an attempt to come up with original solutions that are different from the mainstream.

A synthesizing creative solution combines things that already exist into a new entity. An example of this is option number six of the strategic directions, i.e., market shaping, where the idea is to create something completely new, such as a way of use, through the interplay of existing elements. An example of this is the Spotify music platform. A synthesizing solution can also be a case where a company builds a competitive advantage from the "resource bundle" it has.

Ideas that create value

Any assessment of the quality of a creative product must always be weighed against the traditions and practices of the industry. Knowledge of established practices and conventions is always necessary to assess the usefulness and relevance of an idea.

The assessment of creativity is subjective and timebound. What made text messages meaningful is no longer a radical creative idea in this day and age. Finding a balance between a solution that is familiar to the industry and a "better application" developed from the solution is often important. Launching a radical, unexpected idea can take up resources or even raise doubts within the target group. A good example of radical innovation is the alarm system created by Noccela.

Small, incremental reforms can achieve tangible results faster and more effectively. Queen's mega-hit "Bohemian Rhapsody" is an example of a song that has the structure of a rock song with the grandeur of an opera. Cirque du Soleil's performances combine many different elements, including circus, *dance, theatre* and musical styles *from opera to rock*. Kyrö Distillery has successfully combined Finnish ingredients and elements in the production and branding of gin and whisky.

The Company Cases section contains a large number of companies where industries intersect. They are a successful mix of different elements: enough of the old and tried and tested, enough elements familiar from elsewhere – which combine to create something incrementally new.

Eurekas and revelations

In the context of creativity, creative outcomes are often talked about, but in the business context, it is also important to highlight creative work and creative thinking processes that go into achieving an outcome. Intangible ideas and concepts are also creative work.

Creative work that aims for a clear idea is, by its nature, fragmented, unpredictable, and difficult to pin down in a time and place. Even finding or defining a problem can be challenging and require creative thinking.

Eurekas and moments of revelation are often the results of long processes and a lot of thought. A realisation may have come at a particular moment, for example, when vacuuming the living room or packing groceries at the checkout. But without using the subconscious - either consciously or unconsciously - they would not see the light of day.

Finding and identifying problems, not just solving them, is also essential in the search for a competitive advantage. Problem-solving, critical thinking, and adaptability to change are typical of creative thinking and behaviour.

Many companies today are trying to create something new. They're perhaps doing what has been done before – just a little better. More important than just developing a new product is the ability to offer a new and better alternative. From a business perspective, it is, of course, important to assess the quality of creativity and creative solutions from a business perspective. Ultimately, the customer is the judge of the quality of an idea and its final implementation.

 Renewal starts with new ideas because only if you think in a new way can you do things in a new way.

Storbacka, Blomqvist, Dahl, Haeger

What does Professor Alf Rehn think?

Creativity involves challenging what already exists. Creativity and creative thinking are toolkits for creating something new. But at what point in the creative process are we being creative enough? How does creativity feel? Alf Rehn, Professor of Innovation, Design and Management, highlights the heretical.

"In the Middle Ages, the mild penalty for questioning things was confinement under house arrest or expulsion from home. More serious questioning quickly led to torture or death," he says.

Rehn encourages heresy. Of course, the consequences need not be as serious today as they were in the Middle Ages, but the implications can be even greater. With his unique rhetoric, he encourages companies to hire professional heretics. The title of such a person could be Chief Heretical Officer (CHO), for example.

"Heretics are important not because they oppose, but because they can upset the balance of the system and introduce uncertainty into it, which is the basis of all value creation," Rehn says.

COMPETITIVE ADVANTAGE IS AN UMBRELLA TERM FOR CURRENT TRENDS AND MEANS

For a company, a competitive advantage and a business model built on it are game changers. A new business idea also changes the landscape when it becomes a guiding element in the ways and trends that currently drive the organisation.

Throughout history, businesses have been developed with different doctrines. For historical reasons, the doctrines are mainly based on product-oriented thinking. Development is often understood as internal development. In many companies, this means lay-offs and redundancies, often with a cheese slicer in the lead role. Efficiencies have been sought through cost-cutting, new structures, and organisational changes.

Today's management thinking is full of well-meaning isms and doctrines. Many of us have been shot full of holes with them.

Some isms are born just because there are supposed to be some. Some are born out of necessity, and some because someone managed to sell them to the company. The emperor's clothes have been quickly changed, as fresh approaches have been sought in the turmoil of change. It could even be said that there are so many schools of thought that no one can make sense of them. Isms and doctrines are, of course, well-meaning, but they are often more likely to cause confusion than guide the action in a holistic or coherent way.

Today's top list of toolkits and methods includes growth hacking, lean, inbound/outbound, marketing automation, social selling, thought leadership, vision, self-direction, customer experience, digitalisation, change management, and service design. Sales development is a regular on this hit list.

© Vierula Consulting 2024
M. Vierula, *Find Your Market-Oriented Competitive Advantage*,
https://doi.org/10.1007/978-3-031-71663-8_13

Competitive advantage comes in through the back door

All of the above are good and necessary skills. Many companies have found them to be a great help in their operations. But as has been pointed out, they are inherently product-oriented because the company buying them is product-oriented.

Competitive advantage is the most holistic, concrete, and strategic policy choice for an existing company. Therefore, it can be said that for businesses without a competitive advantage, competitive advantage takes precedence over all of the above means. It is difficult to be a thought leader in an industry if you do not have a competitive advantage perspective that could redeem your thought leadership. Companies using HubSpot and other marketing automation toolkits compete for attention with outbound messaging because most of them do not have a competitive advantage thought through. If an advantage were the basis of communication, a company could invest in the quality of communication rather than the quantity.

Customer experience is often judged by the final stage of the experience. The customer has already made a choice about who to work with. But how do you make sure that the customer starts the buying journey with a specific company? Without a competitive advantage, customer experience cannot be managed because it cannot be consistently operationalized. There are plenty of similar products in the world.

The digital sphere is a great toolkit, but can it be used to create a competitive advantage? Certainly. Now, the buzzword is often, "Let's digitalise!" when it should be, "How can we seek a competitive advantage through digital means?" Could the idea of an online shop be based on competitive advantage? Growth hacking would be much more effective if it had a competitive advantage at its core. In turn, change management needs a direction in which to lead change.

The goals, means, and toolkits of development are taken to the next level by putting a competitive advantage at their core. Since competitive advantage is a foreign concept to business life, it comes to this party as an uninvited guest and through the back door (sneaking sideways like a crab). It reshapes the star chart. A competitive advantage is a bright guiding star for the company.

When companies do not focus on competing with each other but rather develop and evolve their products and services in a market-oriented way, a richer and more diverse supply is created. Familiar methods evolve or find completely new uses. The "creative destruction" caused by competitive advantages creates new and better products. It also makes better use of the competence and resources available in companies.

WELL-KNOWN STRATEGY TOOLKITS

A strategy strongly includes the idea of a future direction of the company. A strategy defines what the company wants to achieve, the environment and competitive situation in which the company operates, and the means by which it will create its future. There is a whole range of strategy toolkits for creating a strategy, from developing resources to creating something new.

I will briefly go through them here, based on the book by **Tero Vuorinen**, DEconSc and engineer. I will describe the different categories and present the toolkits that belong to them. In the spirit of the book in your hands, I will explain in more detail the key points of the toolkits that include the perspective of creating something new and developing the resources available in an organisation.

1. Toolkits to improve efficiency

The toolkits in this group aim to improve efficiency and adapt a business to the needs of its customers. The best-known toolkits in this group are the Balanced Score Card and the SWOT analysis. Other toolkits include Taylorism, Lean, and Strategy Maps.

2. Toolkits for creating something new

The toolkits for creating something new represent the opposite view to the toolkits in the previous group. The best-known toolkit is probably the blue ocean strategy.

Blue ocean strategy

The idea behind the blue ocean strategy is to move into areas that have not yet been conquered. In contrast to the blue ocean, the method's developers have also outlined a red ocean strategy, meaning that the sea has turned blood red as a result of fierce competition. The idea is that there is little competition in the blue ocean.

© Vierula Consulting 2024
M. Vierula, *Find Your Market-Oriented Competitive Advantage*,
https://doi.org/10.1007/978-3-031-71663-8_14

Scenario work

A scenario is an outline of various future possibilities, a kind of description and a script based on it. The toolkit has its origins in the world of cinema and theatre. The idea is not to predict the future but to identify different development possibilities. There are two approaches to a scenario:

- an exploratory scenario, outlining the past and present and moving on to the future
- a goal-oriented scenario that guides the creation of visions of the desired future situation.

Weak signals

The success of a business depends on its ability to succeed in the future. Weak signals, various types of messages about market developments, either spoken out loud or otherwise identifiable, are at the heart of the Weak signals toolkit. The method created by Igor Ansoff aims to see further than scenario work.

Co-creation

Co-creation is a toolkit for creating something new, enabled by the digital environment and central to start-ups. Swarm intelligence and crowdsourcing are the models here. The purpose of co-creation is to involve a large number of people in various ways in the design of a product, service, strategy, or outlining parts of them.

John P. Kotter's 8-step change model

Changes in the competitive and business environment, technological advances, and market changes require change – and further change management. The starting point of the toolkit is to find a vision and sell it to "others". The components are creating the right climate, involving everyone in the change, and implementing and sustaining the change.

All the toolkits directed at creating something new – the blue ocean strategy, scenario work, weak signals, co-creation, and Kotter's 8-step change model – are an integral part of the various toolkits presented in this book.

3. Toolkits for resource development

Toolkits for resource development focus on developing the internal resources of an organisation rather than on monitoring external issues. The internal, resource-based perspective and the external, market-oriented search for a competitive advantage work in tandem; competitive advantage can also be found by distilling a company's existing competence.

Effective toolkits for resource development include:

- the learning organisation
- the Kraljic portfolio model
- employer branding
- benchmarking
- the VRIO model.

The learning organisation emphasises the idea that the knowledge and competence within a company and the ability to learn new things are success factors.

The idea behind the **Kraljic portfolio model** is to change the traditional price-focused purchasing activity towards strategic sourcing.

Employer branding is about engaging and motivating staff and developing the employer's image.

Benchmarking is used to analyse an organisation's performance, its competitors, or the best practices in other industries.

The **VRIO model** aims to identify the factors, or resources, within an organisation on which to build a competitive advantage. VRIO is the most comprehensive of the toolkits in this group.

All the perspectives presented by the different toolkits are also synthesised in this book in the chapter *Finding a competitive advantage in your company's resources*.

4. Positioning toolkits

This toolkitkit focuses on monitoring the competitive and operational environment of the company. The toolkits include generic strategies, PESTEL analysis, Porter's Five Forces model, the BCG matrix, and Michael Hunt's strategic groups.

In the book you are holding, the strategy focuses on finding a competitive advantage and putting it at the heart of your strategy. The strategy is built on the advantage. Toolkits help in the search for a competitive advantage, but without creativity, there can be no innovation. As **Tero Vuorinen** aptly describes in his book: *"...that no matter how hard you work on strategy, using the Balanced Scorecard cannot result in ideas such as, 'What if you could shoot pigs with angry birds, or set up a virtual hotel or farm?'"*

That's why we emphasise the importance of ideas and creativity in this context.

It is good to know all the popular toolkits. The toolkits provide a framework for thinking and brainstorming. They bring perspectives to the organisation, both internally and externally, and also from a competitive perspective. Some of the toolkits are, in principle, intended for the strategic work of large companies.

To see close up, sometimes you have to look far away. Once the scenario, environment, competitor, industry, target group, and stakeholder analyses have been performed, it is also a good idea to introduce a positioning toolkit that allows a close-up assessment of the brands operating in the segment and their position and relevance from the perspective of the target groups. What will happen in the segment when we launch this service? How will our competitors react? The positioning toolkit allows you to both assess competitors' actions and analyse the market in more detail.

SUMMARY

- Creating innovation requires creative thinking and creative ideas.

- Without creative breakthroughs, it is not possible to create compelling and significant competitive advantages.

- A competitive advantage is at the heart of strategy. Therefore, it is also a matter for owners, boards, and management. Equally, it affects all staff intimately.

- Strategic marketing skills are core competences of a market-oriented company.

- Internalising this will help you break free from the straitjacket of product-oriented thinking.

- 'Competitive advantage' is the umbrella term for all the many ways in which businesses are now being developed or their sales efforts promoted.

HOW THE TOOLKIT WAS CREATED

Two rocky and winding paths led to the creation of the toolkit. One of the paths is a book on business development that I started writing in 2016. The other path toward the toolkit took the form of the lectures, training sessions, and consultations I gave on integration, communication, marketing, and branding.

The paths are intertwined.

Professor **Don E. Schultz**, a leading expert on integration, has pointed out that companies have various competences: technical, intellectual, tactical, and skill-based. Competence exists at the individual, team, departmental, and business levels. Schultz noted with concern that competence is often dispersed throughout the organisation. Silos within organisations and separate targets for each of them prevent efficiency from being extracted from the competence within the organisation.

No common plot

During training courses, lectures, and consultations, I noticed time and again that the representatives of different functions did not have a common idea of the purpose of the business. It is difficult to integrate functions and promote interplay between them without a definition of what to integrate on or for. I realised that the book I had started to write required deeper content: promoting team play requires a common thread.

Thus was born an idea of a book which would be a game changer.

I wondered what the companies were missing. What is at the heart of successful businesses? Among other things, I started to think about what good business skills are as a competence area. What is their anatomy? What do they consist of? How does this translate in an era of customer relationships, networks, and knowledge work? What kind of an organisation and culture does it require? Strategy literature failed to show what is at the heart of a successful strategy. So, I had to continue my reflections.

According to the industrial-age model, business competence is product-, production-, and price-driven. It is the ability to produce products at low production costs, the ability to manufacture products and trade them, the ability to sell the products and services produced to meet a need.

© Vierula Consulting 2024
M. Vierula, *Find Your Market-Oriented Competitive Advantage*,
https://doi.org/10.1007/978-3-031-71663-8_15

Times were different then. In today's global environment, in an era of relentless hyper-competition, knowledge work and networks, it has to be more than just cutting unit costs and selling products.

Kotler's ball wall as the basis of the toolkit

As a ball wall for my reflections, professor **Philip Kotler** provided an interesting summary of companies and their ability to respond to market changes. According to Kotler, there are four types of companies:

- those who make things happen
- those who look at what is happening and react to it
- those who see change but fail to react
- those who don't notice anything has happened.

The top two groups were the most interesting for the development of the toolkit: those who make things happen and those who look at what happens and react to it. I actively sought out companies that were putting these ideas into practice. What was distinctive about them? Where does "making things happen" stem from? What is it? There were many questions. The idea of creating a competitive advantage toolkit was thus conceived.

Now, a quick fast-forward in thinking and events.

I explored the topic in more detail by taking a deeper look at companies' business ideas and strategies. My studies showed that they were mostly poor or inadequate. I reflected on the anatomy of a good strategy. What is a good strategy? I studied and examined. In the end, the root cause was found to be a competitive advantage. Eureka! The uranium was enriched. If the company doesn't have one, the strategies are "strategy-ish", or half-hearted barrels of empty wishes. I realised that there are two types of companies:

- those without a competitive advantage
- those with a competitive advantage

I realised that being a digital agency or a café is not a competitive advantage and that a law firm is not a business idea as such.

Colours came into my world

So, I looked at the competitive advantage at the heart of successful businesses. The lights came on, colours came into my world. Of course. When there is more supply than demand, a company needs to create something superior. When we already have everything we need, no one lacks anything as easily as before. When no one can expect anything better, a company needs to create something new that is compelling and meaningful.

The importance of competitive advantage as a key success factor is highlighted by studies, professors, white papers, literature, consultants, gurus, articles, and successful business leaders. Competitive advantage emerges as a key element in business ideas, business models, company strategies, and management.

But how do you create a market-oriented competitive advantage? I could not find any toolkits to develop it, which was surprising in itself, given the importance of competitive advantage as a business success factor.

The idea of a toolkit tantalized me and drove me to create one

I became increasingly excited by the idea of developing a toolkit for finding a competitive advantage. I wondered if the "differentiating factor" could be created from the business idea of a company. I considered the difference between the "sales + marketing" and "marketing + desire to buy" perspectives. During my journey of a few years, I had a few major insights while the developing the toolkit, but for the most part, the evolution of my thinking and the development of the toolkit progressed in small steps. In the training sessions I held, I perhaps realised one thing, in a meeting, another, and in a seminar, a third that combined my two previous realisations into a bigger picture.

Dozens of definitions

In planning the toolkit, I went through dozens of different definitions of marketing. I tried to find a definition that was neither channel- nor product-oriented but rather market-oriented. I discussed this with several people. The keyword, or more precisely two words, was strategic marketing. I was familiar with marketing. Professor Philip Kotler's definition of strategic marketing was selected as the framework of the toolkit.

The classic 4P model, with all its different versions, felt old-fashioned. It was based on product orientation. Marketing was basically seen as marketing communication. Where was the deeper meaning of marketing? That is, the meaning that targets strategic decisions within the company and not marketing communications aimed at influencing target groups.

The term 'strategic' referred to big, crucial policy decisions. What are the dimensions behind and at the heart of the word strategy? It's a mysterious word that was difficult to get a grip on.

The most challenging level of learning is challenging your own thinking. I pondered the idea that product-oriented thinking has become a mental straitjacket for companies. That mindset should be broken and reformed. To think in a new way, you need to renew the starting points of your thinking. You have to know what you don't know.

Searching for companies

I started looking for companies that clearly had "their thing": a competitive advantage, a business idea, a clear and distinctive strategy, a mission or vision. What I found is that, indeed, very few companies have a competitive advantage or a strategy based on competitive advantage.

I also found a whole bunch of exceptions, Finnish companies that clearly had "their thing". I took down their good business ideas. The flimsy or conventional ones (those identical to ideas offered by competitors) I put in the bio waste bin. I analysed the good ones and sorted them into different categories. The toolkit's strategic guidelines and the three different definitions of competitive advantage were generated by modelling business ideas on the competitive advantages of these outstanding companies.

The ABC method as the basis of the toolkit

The toolkit is based on a kind of ABC method, where A stands for academic, broad-based literature. B stands for business cases where I have been part of a team, either as a consultant, leader, or listener. C stands for communication, which in practice meant talking with professionals and representatives of different functions in different contexts as an instructor, consultant, or lecturer.

Creating the toolkit was a matter of reducing and modelling reality. In order to create the toolkit, theory and frameworks were needed. On the other hand, to put theory into practice, practical business solutions and living business life were needed. The toolkit evolved through several phases. Along the way, I had the opportunity to showcase versions of the toolkit at events large and small. I maintained a dialogue between theory and practice. The toolkit was received enthusiastically at all stages. I felt that the idea was understood – and that it comes in response to a considerable need.

We live in an era of communality. The idea of competition between companies seemed old-fashioned and stale to me. This is also because a company operating in a modern environment is increasingly collaborating with competitors. This idea that direct competition between companies is useless is also discussed by Simon Sinek in The Infinite Game (2018). He stresses the idea that a chess or football match are games where a clear winner is sought. Operation between businesses is a constant chain of new games because there is no final winner. Successful businesses are those that can innovate and create meaning.

When companies primarily compete with each other, two outcomes result: one wins, and the others lose. If you keep your eye on the competition, you can't create something new and interesting. In production-oriented thinking, the focus is on the company's portfolio, while in market-oriented thinking, it is on the needs of customers – or even customers' customers.

Innovation is the driving force behind economic growth and development. New products challenge old products and ways of thinking, and the resulting "creative chaos" opens the way for development. I think companies should compete with each other to create something new and superior rather than fight each other for customers.

Why on earth should I be the one to make perhaps the first and only "find your competitive advantage" toolkit in the world? I thought that my background as a strategist, creative designer, copywriter, creative director, and entrepreneur lent itself to the development of the toolkit. Creative thinking is an essential skill in creating something new. After all, I had been developing my country's leading brands, creating new services for them, taking Finnish brands to international markets, helping companies, organisations, and municipalities to create and clarify their brands, taking the Finnish summer and Finnish winter to four continents, productizing, writing various missions, strategies, and so on. Hundreds and hundreds of assignments where positioning and differentiation were often achieved through marketing communications.

My own career has mostly consisted of creative work for commercial purposes. I have created marketing concepts, designed marketing communications for both individual and multiple channels, written slogans and radio scripts, developed beer and mineral water concepts, positioned products and services, written press releases, created marketing plans and strategies.

Assignments are based on scientific, operational, emotional, and commercial objectives. I know from experience that it takes a different skill set to position a beer brand and create a certain image for it through advertising than it does to support the sales efforts of an ice-breaking cruiser or to communicate the features of a telehandler to its user and those involved in the purchase decision.

My work has also brought in a fair share of prizes, both nationally and internationally. After celebrating the awards, I always took the time to analyse why a campaign or operation had been successful. My previous books and the practical experience gained from them were essential to the creation of the toolkit. Without them, I would not have been able to create the toolkit.

I felt that I had the right combination of theoretical knowledge, curiosity, stubbornness, courage, analytical thinking, a generalist approach, and creative skills to justify myself as a toolkit developer.

If you think you're too small to have an impact, try going to bed with a mosquito.

Anita Roddick, founder of Body Shop

I've also gained valuable experience from being on the ground, so to speak; I've been involved as an owner, founder, and manager of several businesses. I have succeeded, and I have failed. My career in marketing agencies has given me insight into dozens and dozens of industries and hundreds of products and services. The different areas of business have become familiar.

"I'll have to give it a try," I mused. "Anything can happen."

At some point, I "reached" a point where thinking about competitive advantage took over. I saw all products, services, and businesses only through their competitive advantage. I was exposed to a manic onslaught of competitive advantages. I can say I went to bed with the concept and even felt I woke up with it. Maybe I also ate with it because I was analysing everything through it. I read everything from fiction to fact through it.

The classic 4P model, which outlines the role of marketing, focused on one or two Ps in too many companies. It was often just outbound communication. Where was strategic marketing? And what is it all about? The modern era has created new perspectives and books that discuss these perspectives, such as Jim Collins' *Good to Great*, *Blue Ocean Strategy*, Simon Sinek's *Why* and Frederic Laloux's *Reinventing Organizations* (2014). The *Business Model Canvas* provided a platform on which to build a business model. I realised I had to stand on the shoulders of giants – and reach for the next level. I realised that a conscious focus on finding a competitive advantage had been overlooked.

The reason, of course, is that consciously developing a competitive advantage is challenging. If it were easy, there would be many more companies with a competitive advantage. The same phenomenon can be seen, for example, in hit songs. There are far more talented people trying to create a hit song than there are hit songs.

You can order your company's visual identity or slogan online. However, a competitive advantage cannot be bought on the web. You can't google a competitive advantage. It doesn't arise through artificial intelligence: It needs to be created.

The Find Your Competitive Advantage toolkit eventually grew into a toolkit. At its core, there are seven strategic directions and three definitions of competitive advantage. In addition to these, toolkits were also developed on topics such as how to start looking for a competitive advantage. The result was a toolkit to assess the quality of a competitive advantage and a toolkit to assess the starting point for a company to create a competitive advantage. The resources available in a company are also a toolkit for clarifying the competitive advantage. The toolkit also includes toolkits for planning communications.

From toolkit to book

Many people have asked why I chose not to keep the toolkit just to myself for use in my own company. Many people have pointed out that it's easy to steal. But many people also know I have invested a lot of resources in it. The decision to publish the toolkit as a book was born quickly. I wanted to use the open-source principle. In other words, a toolkit is at its best when others are using it. I think that businesses, and therefore societies, need businesses with the ability to produce better added value.

And why an English-language book as well? This is an abridged and supplemented version of the Finnish book. There are two reasons for publishing the international version:

- There is no comparable book and toolkit available.
- After the book was published, I received enquiries and encouragement to write an English version as well.

The book has received profuse praise. It has been called a masterpiece, the best business book of the year. I did not mind it being called a world-class work. The second edition appeared less than a year after the book was published. Academic acceptance has also been achieved: a Finnish business school provides a B.Sc. course titled Competitive Advantage from Market Orientation that uses a Finnish version of this book as course material. The course book is the Finnish version.

A FINE CONCLUSION TO THE TOOLKIT

Development and growth are based on the creation of something new. In order for something new to emerge, I have stubbornly sought to challenge the prevailing ideas about the starting point for doing business. I have replaced them with the idea of market-oriented thinking. I have explored different perspectives and delved deep into strategic horizons. I have immersed myself in strategic marketing, which can rightly be said to be the driving force, heart, and brain behind this book. Strategic marketing has been a pervasive driving force without being actively raised as a buzzword.

At this point on my long path, it seems that internalising strategic marketing was the Gordian knot that needed to be untied. It helped me open up market-oriented thinking. It enabled the creation of the Find Your Competitive Advantage™ toolkit.

Competitive advantage is a term mentioned more often in this book than in truckloads of strategy literature. I believe that my book does what I am talking about: the creation of radical innovation. I'm talking about radical innovation. Therefore, it may also cause resistance and denial. Or it might only inspire a certain group of people. It has already done its job by ensuring that the reader understands the concept and meaning of competitive advantage. I believe that this realisation will trigger the idea of searching for something new. Or the idea that a company will not be content to do what its competitors do.

Finding a competitive advantage is not easy. But to encourage you, I would like to quote **Michelangelo**, the architect, the sculptor, the poet, the artist. When asked how he managed to create the statue of David, he is said to have replied that it was inside that slab of stone. It's worth starting to look for your own David. Ambition is a good driver. The customer's perspective is the most important. What you like is not essential. You have to think that even if you like wild strawberries, when fishing you should offer Rapala lures.

© Vierula Consulting 2024
M. Vierula, *Find Your Market-Oriented Competitive Advantage*,
https://doi.org/10.1007/978-3-031-71663-8_16

You don't become a customer's best friend by pulling a rabbit out of a hat. You need to find a solution that appeals to your customers. Not everyone can create Solar Foods, Amazon, Benecol, or Wolt. But every product, service, and organisation has the right and the capacity to find a competitive advantage.

Strategy as a term has been mystified. As a simple person, I think that success can only be based on the value you bring to your customers. And that there is a competitive advantage behind a successful business idea.

I wish you the best of luck in your quest for a competitive advantage!

Author and developer of the toolkit

Markku Vierula, Executive MBA, publicist and journalist, is an author, consultant, lecturer, creative leader, entrepreneur, and board professional. He has had a successful career as a copywriter, creative director, member of management teams and boards of directors, founder, and owner of leading marketing agencies in Finland and around the world.

Vierula's work has won numerous awards in both Finnish and international competitions. He has also been on the jury of several competitions. His long career in marketing agencies has given him the opportunity to gain a broad and comprehensive understanding of a wide range of industries, companies, professions, and cultures. He feels that without his marketing experience and profound knowledge of integration, as well as his experience of the interplay between marketing, sales, and communications gained during consultancy and training, he would not have been able to take a sufficiently in-depth look at strategic marketing and the development of a competitive advantage toolkit.

Vierula is also the author of an integration book called Suuri integraatiokirja - markkinointi, myynti ja viestintä (2014), which is also used as a textbook and course book for universities and colleges.

www.vierula.com
Markku@vierula.com

Thanks

There are many talented people behind this book and toolkit. First of all, thanks to all the companies presented here. Surging Mexican waves to you all. You are exemplary. You are an inspiration. Thanks to Mailis Kriikku for the graphic ideas. Professor Hannu Makkonen, warm thanks for sparring and discussing the toolkit. Thanks to Tero Vuorinen, DEconSc and engineer, for the reading tips. Thank you for your cooperation, Timo Lappi from Heltti. Thanks to Taina Parviainen and Mikko Puranen for the collaboration that led to the book. A big thank you to strategist Marco Mäkinen for his encouragement.

Hats off also to the social media and the business leaders and owners, marketing, communications, HR, ICT, and sales communities and professionals with whom I had the opportunity to discuss the themes of the book.

Football is always to be thanked. Practising, playing, and looking for line-breaking passes were the only moments when I wasn't thinking about this toolkit and book.

Thanks also to the driver of this book: strategic marketing.
Helsinki, Finland, July 2024

Markku Vierula

SOURCE LIST

Articles and literature sources

Ahto O., Kahri A., Kahri T., Mäkinen M.: Bulkista brändiksi – Käsikirja kasvuun ja kannattavuuteen. Docendo 2016.

Barney J.: Firm Resources and Sustained Competitive Advantage. Journal of Management, 17(1): 99-120. 1991.

Brandenburger A.: Strategy Needs Creativity. Harvard Business Review, March-April 2019. Downloadable https://hbr. org/2019/03/strategy-needs-creativity?utm_campaig

Chan W., Kim, Mauborgne R.; R.: Sinisen meren strategia. Alma Talent 2015.

Chan W., Kim, Mauborgne R.: Uusi sininen meri – Rohkeus kasvaa. Alma Talent 2017.

Chan W., Kim, Mauborgne R.: Beyond Disruption. Harvard Business Review Press 2023.

Clark D.: If Strategy Is So Important, Why Don't We Make Time for It? Harvard Business Review, 21.6.2018. Downloadable https://hbr.org/2018/06/if-strategy-is-so- important-why-dont-we-make-time-for-it

Collins J.: Hyvästä paras. Alma Talent 2002.

de Chernatory L.: From brand vision to brand evaluation: strategically building and sustaining brands. Butterworth Heinemann 2002.

Grönroos C.: Palvelujen johtaminen ja markkinointi. Alma Talent 2015.

Hakanen M.: PK-yrityksen strategiatyö tutuksi. Benchmarking 2012.

Hamel G., Prahalad C.: Competing for the Future. Harvard Business School Press 1996.

Heinonen V., Konttinen H.: Nyt uutta Suomessa! – Suomalaisen mainonnan historia. Mainostajien liitto 2001.

Heiskanen A.: Tietoisesti taitava myynnin johtaja. Alma Talent 2019.

Hämäläinen V., Maula H., Suominen K.: Digiajan strategia. Alma Talent 2016.

Ilmarinen V., Koskela K.: Digitalisaatio – Yritysjohdon käsikirja. Alma Talent 2015.

Järvilehto P., Järvilehto L.: Pim! Olet luova. Tuuma 2019.

Kamensky M., Strateginen johtaminen. Menestyksen timantti. Talentum 2010.

Keronen K., Tanni K.: Johdata asiakkaasi verkkoon: opas koukuttavan sisältöstrategian luomiseen. Alma Talent 2013.

Korkiakoski K.: Asiakaskokemus ja henkilöstökokemus. Alma Talent 2019.

Korkiakoski K., Gerdt B.: Ylivoimainen asiakaskokemus: työkalupakki. Alma Talent 2016.

Korpijaakko M., Nuutinen H.: Merkkejä maineesta: tarinoita suomalaisista brändeistä. Heikki Nuutinen Design & Smart Communication 2020.

Koskinen P.: Vain prosentilla yrityksistä on hyvä strategia - "Kannattava kasvu ei ole strategia". Kauppalehti 9.12.2018. Downloadable from https://www.kauppalehti.fi/ uutiset/vain-prosentilla-yrityksista-on-hyva-strategia- kannattava-kasvu-ei-ole-strategia/755bdffa-2ee5-43fc-9812- c7cb999cb4e6

Kotler P.: Markkinoinnin avaimet – 80 konseptia menestykseen. readme.fi 2005.

Kotler P., Kartajaya H., Setiawan I.: Markkinointi 3.0. Alma Talent 2011.

Kurkilahti L, Äijö T.: Yritysten strategiat ovat hukassa. Talouselämä Tebatti 12.10.2014. Downloadable from https:// www.talouselama.fi/uutiset/yritysten-strategiat-ovat- hukassa/2d097b11-aa4d-3d8f-a14a-cbadc65452fb

Laakso H.: Brändit kilpailuetuna: miten rakennan ja kehitän tuotemerkkiä. Alma Talent 2003.

Lahti A.: Markkinointi kilpailuetuna. International Networking Publishing INP 1993.

Lahti A.: Yrityksen kilpailustrategia. Ekonomia-sarja 1983.

Laloux F.: Reinventing organizations: a guide to creating organizations inspired by the next the of human consciousness. Nelson Parker 2014.

Lempiälä T., Näsänen J., Vanharanta O.: Muutos ei synny pintaremontilla. Talouselämä Tebatti 20.8.2015. Downloadable from https://www.talouselama.fi/uutiset/muutos- ei-synny-pintaremontilla/ddc75ea6-cacc-3336-ab68- 30fc45676fcf

Lindberg-Repo K., Mehra E., Gupta N., Dube A., Kaul V.: Titans of branding, CERS 2009

Luukka P.: Yrityskulttuuri on kuningas: mikä, miksi ja miten? Alma Talent 2019.

Malmelin N.: Radikaali uudistuminen – miten johtaa murroksessa. Kauppakamari 2021.

Malmelin N., Hakala J.: Radikaali brändi. Alma Talent 2007.

Malmelin N., Poutanen P.: Luovuuden idea: luovuus työelämässä, yhteisöissä ja organisaatioissa. Gaudeamus 2017.

Mattila, P. & Rautiainen, M. Putki: Johda markkinointia ja myyntiä yhdessä. Talentum 2010.

Melgin E. (toim.): Blogtalk, kirjoituksia työelämästä ja viestinnästä. ProCom –viestinnän ammattilaiset ry 2019.

Mäkinen M., Kahri A., Kahri T.: Brändi kulmahuoneeseen. Sanoma Pro Oy 2010.

Neilimo K., Näsi J.: Mitä on liiketoimintaosaaminen. WSOYpro 2008.

Nenonen S., Storbacka K.: Markkinamuotoilu: johdatko markkinoita vai johtavatko markkinat sinua? WSOYPro, 2010.

Nenonen S., Storbacka K.: SMASH: Using Market Shaping to Design New Strategies for Innovation, Value Creation, and Growth. Emerald Publishing Limited 2018.

Otala L.: Osaamispääoman johtamisesta kilpailuetu. WSOYpro 2008.

Paananen L.: Hallitus ja markkinointi. Alma Talent 2009.

Parantainen J.: Tuotteistaminen – Rakenna palvelusta menestystuote 10 päivässä. Alma Talent 2007.

Piha K.: Rytmihäiriö – Tartu mahdollisuuksiin tai kuole. AlmaTalent 2015.

Piha K.: Konflikti päivässä, kulttuuri ratkaisee yrityksen kohtalon, Alma Talent 2017.

Porter Michael E.: Kilpailuetu: miten ylivoimainen osaaminen luodaan ja säilytetään. Weilin + Göös 1988.

Porter Michael E.: Competitive Advantage, creating and sustaining superior performance. Free Press 2004.

Rehn A.: Vaaralliset ideat. Kun sopimaton ajattelu on tärkein voimavarasi. Alma Talent 2010.

Ries A: Positioning – The Battle for Your Mind, McGraw-Hill 2001.

Ries E.: Lean startup – kokeilukulttuurin käsikirja. LavasDesign Oy 2016.

Rope T.: Johdon markkinointiratkaisut: strateginen markkinointi. WSOY 2003.

Rope T.: Suuri markkinointikirja. Kauppakaari 2000.

Rope T.: Voita markkinoinnilla. Kauppakamari 2011.

Ruokolainen P.: Brändikäsikirja. Kauppakamari 2020.

Santalainen T.: Strateginen ajattelu ja toiminta. Alma Talent 2009.

Santalainen T.: Strateginen ajattelu. Alma Talent 2014.

Schulz D., Schulz H.: IMC, The Next Generation. McGraw-Hill Books 2003.

Scott D.: The New Rules Of Marketing and PR. John Wiley & Sons, Inc 2010.

Sinek S.: Start with why: how great leaders inspire everyone to take action, Portfolio Penguin 2009.

Sinek S.: The Infininite Game. Penguin Business 2019

Storbacka K., Dahl J., Blomqvist R., Haeger T.: Asiakkuuden arvon lähteillä. WSOY 2003.

Tikkanen H., Frösen J.: StratMark II: strategisen markkinoinnin teho ja tulokset. Alma Talent, 2010.

Tikkanen H, Vassinen A.: Stratmark: strateginen markkinointiosaaminen. Alma Talent 2010.

Torkkola S.: Lean asiantuntijatyön johtamisessa. Alma Talent 2016.
Trout J., Hafren G.: Erilaistu tai kuole. Edita Publishing Oy 2003.
Tuominen K.: Strategia 2013: itsearvioinnin työkirja: 50 hyvää kysymystä ja esimerkkiparia. Benchmarking Ltd Oy 2012.
Typpö A.: Läpimurto on vielä tekemättä. Kauppalehti 13.1.2017. Downloadable from https://www.kauppalehti.fi/ uutiset/ lapimurto-on-viela-tekematta/98ae2698-7878- 3420-b435- 7c0896a08eb4?utm_source=marmai&utm_ medium= almainternal&utm_campaign=mm_redirect
Uusitalo P.: Brändi & business. Mainostajien liitto 2014.
Vahtola M.: Intohimona brändit – Kolme vuosikymmentä brändien parissa. Docendo 2020.
Vermeulen F.: Many Strategies Fail Because They're Not Actually Strategies 8.11.2017 Harvard Business Review. Downloadable from https://hbr-org.cdn.ampproject.org/c/s/hbr. org/amp/2017/11/many-strategies-fail-because-theyre-not- actually-strategies
Vierula M.: Suuri integraatiokirja – Markkinointi, myynti, viestintä. Alma Talent 2014.
Vierula M.: Täällä luuraa strateginen markkinointi. Kauppalehti 24.1.2017. Downloadable from https://www. kauppalehti.fi/uutiset/taalla-luuraa-strateginen- markkinointi/732a64bd-3d02-30e7-a9ef-d84031191752?utm_ source=marmai&utm_medium=almainternal&utm_ campaign=mm_redirect&proxy=uutiset/ taalla-luuraa-strateginen-markkinointi/732a64bd-3d02-30e7- a9ef-d84031191752
Vierula M.: Hyvä viestintästrategia edellyttää parempia strategioita. Viestijät.fi-verkkosivut 4.12.2018. Downloadable from https://viestijat.fi/hyva-strategiaviestinta-edellyttaa-parempia- strategioita/#884d7739
Vierula M.: Markkinointikeskustelusta puuttuu strategisen markkinoinnin ulottuvuus. Kauppalehti 7.10.2019. Downloadable from https://www.kauppalehti.fi/uutiset/markkinointikeskustelusta-puuttuu-strategisen-markkinoinnin-ulottuvuus/e50081d2-8a5b-4a73-949e-19ad6b7c9e8e?utm_ source= marmai&utm_medium=almainternal&utm_ campaign=mm_redirect
Viita H.: Arvoa liiketoimintaan – Brändin lanseeraus vuodessa. Alma Talent 2020
Vuorinen T.: Verkostot organisoitumisen muotona: hermeneuttinen analyysi kahdenvälisten suhteiden rakentumisesta kärkiyrityskontekstissa. Vaasan yliopisto 2005. Downloadable from http://urn.fi/URN:NBN:fi-fe2018060725545
Vuorinen T.: Strategiakirja: 20 työkalua. Alma Talent 2013.

Vuorinen T., Hakala H., Kohtamäki M., Uusitalo K.: Mapping the landscape of strategy tools: A review on strategy tools published in leading journals within the past 25 years. LUT University 2017. Downloadable from https://research.lut.fi/ converis/portal/Publication/10359620?auxfun=&lang=en_GB

Ylä-Anttila A.: Tutkimus: suomalaisten pk-yritysten markkinointipanostukset ovat vaatimattomia – "Tarvitaan iso muutos ajatteluun". Kauppalehti 15.1.2019. Downloadable from https://www.kauppalehti.fi/uutiset/tutkimus- suomalaisten-pk-yritysten-markkinointipanostukset-ovat-vaatimattomia-tarvitaan-iso-muutos-ajatteluun/99f8e69b- fd7b-370e-813c-a666abd5fc53?utm_source=marmai&utm_ medium= almainternal&utm_campaign=mm_redirect

Zohar D.: Rewiring the Corporate Brain. Berreth-Koehler publishers 1997.

Blog sources

Aura O.: Strategia pk-yrityksissä. Auran faktat blogi 24.4.2018. Downloadable from https://www.ossiaura.com/auran-faktat-blogi/strategia-pk-yrityksissa

Iivari S.: Viestinnäntekijät ovat nyt kiireisempiä kuin koskaan – ja se on hyvä se. 20.5.2020 Ellun Kanat. Downloadable from https://ellunkanat.fi/nakemys/artikkelit/viestinnantekijat-ovat- nyt-kiireisempia-kuin-koskaan-ja-se-on-hyva-se/

Jarenko K: Unohda perinteinen urasuunnittelu – ketteryys tuli myös urajohtamiseen. Filosofian Akatemia 9.2.2021. Downloadable from https://filosofianakatemia.fi/kirjoittaja/karoliina- jarenko/

Mäkinen M.: On helpompi kuolla kuin muuttua. Digitalist Network 9.1.2015. Downloadable from https://digitalist.global/ talks/helpompi-kuolla-kuin-muuttua/

https://seths.blog/

Saarijärvi H.: Näkökulmia markkinoinnin evoluutioon ja revoluutioon. Tampereen yliopisto 5.11.2018. Downloadable from https://blogs.tuni.fi/vaikuttaja/kauppatieteet/nakokulmia-markkinoinnin-evoluutioon-ja-revoluutioon/

Events, discussions and interviews

Hyytiälä H., Niemi, A.: Miten johtaa ketterää organisaatiota? Tilaisuuden järjestäjä: Gofore 17.12.2020. Viewable https://gofore.com/tapahtuma/miten-johtaa- ketteraa-organisaatiota/

Jarenko K.: Tulevaisuudessa menestyvät vain ne organisaatiot, jotka osaavat johtaa työntekijöiden sisäistä motivaatiota ja itseohjautuvuutta. Mainostorstai-tapahtuma Turussa 27.2.2020.

Kostiainen J.: Erilaistu tai kuole; kulttuuri, osallisuus ja johtajuus aluekehityksessä.

Esitys Satakunta-päivässä 31.8.2012.
Downloadable from https://www.slideshare.net/SitraFund/erilaistu-tai-kuole- kulttuuri-osallisuus-ja-johtajuus-aluekehityksess

Lukuisat keskustelut Jyväskylän yliopiston väitöskirjatutkija Salla Syväsen kanssa mentori–aktori-roolissa vuonna 2020.

Sarasvuo J.: "Tarvitsemme yritysten johtoon osaamiseen perustuvaa riskinottoa." Haastateltava Jari Sarasvuo, haastattelija Jaakko Tapaninen. Rytminmuutos-tapahtuma 30.8.2016. Viewable https://www.youtube.com/watch?v=zj9Fbzqbd_8

Studies and reports

Deloitte. Nordic CMO -tutkimus, syyskuu 2017.

Sailas R., Virtanen E., Skog H., Pursiainen H.: Entä jos...-
Näkökulmia ja ideoita innovatiivisen hallinnon rakentamiseen. Valtiovarainministeriön julkaisuja 41/2011.
Downloadable from https://vm.fi/documents/10623/1170760/ Ent%C3%A4+jos_N%C3%A4k%C3%B6kulmia+ja+ideoita+innovatiivisen+hallinnon+rakentamiseen_julkaisu+41b_2011. pdf/a1f3931e-86e7-4ffb-8ec9-5d03e57ec815

World Economic Forum. Global Competitiveness Index 2017-2018 -tutkimus. The Global Competitiveness Report 2017-2018.
Downloadable from http://reports.weforum.org/global-competitiveness-index-2017-2018/

Web sources

Esa, M.: Strategia vastaa tärkeään kysymykseen – Älä suhtaudu siihen ylimielisesti. Y-studio.fi 20.5. 2021. Downloadable from https://y-studio.fi/yrityksen-kasvu/johtaminen/strategia-vastaa-tarkeaan-kysymykseen/

Harva työntekijä ymmärtää työpaikkansa strategiaa. Vaasan yliopiston verkkosivut 14.4.2016. Downloadable from https://www.univaasa.fi/fi/news/maury/

Hyytiälä H., Virtanen, P.: Mitä jos valtionhallinto siirtyisi tapauskohtaiseen organisoitumiseen? Sitran verkkosivut 11.1.2019. Downloadable from https://www.sitra.fi/ artikkelit/mita-jos-valtionhallinto-siirtyisi-tapauskohtaiseen- organisoitumiseen

Jarenko K.: Tältä näyttää itseohjautuvuuden kehittäminen suomalaisilla työpaikoilla. Filosofian akatemia -verkkosivut 11.2.2020. Downloadable from https://filosofianakatemia. fi/blogi/talta-nayttaa-itseohjautuvuuden-kehittaminen- suomalaisilla-tyopaikoilla/

Jarenko K.: Barbapapa-organisaatioiden maihinnousu! – Itseohjautuvuus on keino toteuttaa yrityksen strategiaa. Bonfire 13.8.2020. Downloadable from https://www. bonfire.fi/barbapapa-organisaatioiden-maihinnousu- itseohjautuvuus-on-keino-toteuttaa-yrityksen-strategiaa/

Markkinoinnin edistämiskeskus Makes: https://makes.fi/

Martin R.: The Difference Between a Good and Bad Strategy, TKP CLIPS 2022. Downloadable www.youtube.com/watch?v=8cGY8JLdUc8

Martin R.: A Plan Is Not a Strategy, Harward Business Revie 2022. Downloadable https://www.youtube.com/watch?v=iuYlGRnC7J8s

Rytkönen S.: Markkinointi voi surkeasti Suomessa. Myynnin & Markkinoinnin Ammattilaiset -verkkosivut 12.4.2017. Downloadable from https://mma.fi/ajankohtaista/ artikkelit/markkinointi-voi-surkeasti-suomessa/

The Helsinki term bank for the arts and sciences:
https://tieteentermipankki.fi/wiki/Kasvatustieteet: liikeidea
https://tieteentermipankki.fi/wiki/Kasvatustieteet: kilpailuetu

Turunen, Joonas: Nastolassa valmistetut työpöydät vietiin käsistä, Varusteleka löi läpi Pohjois-Amerikassa – Osa yrityksistä onnistui kasvamaan korona-aikana. Helsingin Sanomat 7.9.2020. Downloadable from https://www.hs.fi/talous/ art-2000006626670.html

Äijö, E.: EK huolissaan: Talous kasvaa, mutta pk-yritysten tavoitteet eivät. Yle uutiset 15.6.2017. Downloadable from https://yle. fi/uutiset/3-9671353

THE BOOK BLURBS

I am impressed with Markku Vierula's thought provoking marketing book that aims to help you find a sound marketing strategy for your offering. He supplies more than 40 tools and plenty of examples of companies that have successfully found their market oriented competitive advantage. Do your best to present your target customers with a clear and compelling value proposition that is better or at least different from your competitors.

Professor Philip Kotler
S.C.Johnson Distinguished Professor of International Marketing,
Kellogg School of Management, Northwestern University

Your customers need clarity, they need to know why they should choose you over your competitors. Markku Vierula's book helps you achieve this clarity. It tells you why you need a strategic competitive advantage, how do you come up with one, and, most importantly, how do you deliver on it. When you want to stand out, create a category of one, and generate profits on a much higher level, you need to read this book, and put it's concrete tips into action.

Marco Mäkinen
Chief Strategy Officer, TBWA\Helsinki

Markku Vierula's book pleasantly provides a comprehensive strategic insight into the core of marketing. No frills, no unnecessary details, no gimmicks. The book is concise, essential, and beneficial for every entrepreneur, as well as for all employees in various organizations. I warmly recommend it to students as well; it offers not only a valuable marketing philosophy but also provides practical tools to live by it in the business world.

Professor Jaana Tähtinen
Professor of Marketing
Turku School of Economics, University of Turku

Competitive advantage – all companies need one, and most CEOs are still looking for it. Finding and holding onto the right way to compete for your specific organization can be a daunting task, but thankfully Markku Vierula has provided the world with his manual! This is a comprehensive toolbox of ways to think about and act upon your company's core strategic questions, complete with a broad range of examples from successful Finnish engagements with the key business quandary of our age. A book to read and then to live out!

Professor Alf Rehn
Professor of Innovation, Design, and Management
University of Southern Denmark

This is an excellent book for understanding what you're missing and why your business isn't growing. Or realizing what you may already have but haven't understood to refine into your superpower.

Only 10% of listed companies are genuinely profitable investments. They are, by definition, companies with a competitive advantage.

This is a great textbook on the fundamental difference between competitive advantage and competitiveness.

Kari Tervonen
Roadmap Director Omnicom Media Group

Markku Vierula's latest work tackles perhaps the most fundamental issue in building business success: competitive advantage. No business can be successful without one. With insightful expertise, Vierula opens readers to multiple perspectives from which unique competitive advantages can be forged. His approach, combining strategic marketing with real-world examples, provides essential guidance for those striving to secure a leading edge in their industry.

Pasi Aaltola
Director of MBA Education
University of Jyväskylä

This book gives everyone the opportunity to understand the deepest essence of companies, or to realize that it is missing. The world's pace of development is accelerating and new companies and brands are being created more than anyone needs. With the help of this book and the lessons, you can contribute to the fact that the company and brand you manage or own is vibrant despite all the turmoil. The book works both for those interested in entrepreneurship and business life, as well as for connoisseurs. If you want to play in the winners team, read this!

Sanna Laakkio
CEO
The Association of Finnish Marketers

If you are or want to be a game changer in your organisation and want to create or develop a brand that is future fit, this book is a must-have. Concrete examples and tools will help to take your brand's next steps. With the book you will find differentiating ways to cut to the chosen market. Inspiring and helpful, strategic but practical. Luv it!

Samppa Vilkuna
CEO & Founder
superson.co

Competitive advantage is something that all companies and brands are searching for but unfortunately only a few really have found it. This book gives practical instructions and great tools to create a real competitive advantage and tells what it requires. Great guide for marketing, business management and CEOs."

Riitta Salenius-Mela
Director, Marketing and Portfolio Management
Vice President, Portfolio and Brands
Kekkilä-BVB

With a seemingly small change, a whole new world opens up. In the best case scenario, an entire business can be turned completely upside down. The competitive advantage Markku Vierula describes in his book redefines the factors that matter most. The book is practical, well-structured and clear. It guides the reader in creating a radically new competitive advantage that is market oriented.

Hannu Suokivi
Educator and consultant, MD of Solar Simulator

Vierula's book underscores the pivotal role of a well-defined brand and organizational unity in effective communication. By fostering collaboration and alignment, the book empowers change leaders to communicate ideas internally and to the market. With insightful analysis and practical tools, it equips them to leverage competitive advantages, fostering sustainable growth in today's competitive digitally driven landscape. A must-read for change leaders in the digital transformation era, navigating complexities and driving innovation.

Merita Vilen
Organizational Change Management Program Manager
HCL America Inc.